HUNTER–POINTER–RETRIEVER: THE CONTINENTAL GUNDOG

HUNTER-POINTER-RETRIEVER:

THE CONTINENTAL GUNDOG

Edited by Tony Jackson

Illustrations by Marion Jones

Ashford
Southampton
1989

Published by Ashford, 1 Church Road, Shedfield, Hampshire SO3 2HW

The authors and publisher would like to extend their thanks to the Kennel Club for granting permission to reproduce the breed standard for the six HPR breeds.

British Library Cataloguing in Publication Data
Jackson, Tony, *1937–*
    The Hunter Pointer Retriever.
    1. Gundogs. Hunter pointer retrievers
    I. Title
    636.7'52

    ISBN 1-85253-189-4

Typeset by Acorn Bookwork, Salisbury, Wiltshire
Printed in Great Britain

CONTENTS

INTRODUCTION

Tony Jackson

A brisk afternoon in late January. The Welney Washes, that haunt of
wigeon and pintail, are sprinkled with light flashes of water and
a brisk wind is blowing from the North Sea. We are working
the German short-haired pointer through the reed-beds and dyke
edges of these Cambridgeshire marshes, seeking those elusive wild
pheasants, direct descendants, I swear, of the first birds released in
Britain. Was it by the Romans or Normans?

And with me is my host who tells me that he has yet to shoot over a
hunter-pointer-retriever and who finds himself expressing sheer
amazement at the facility with which the old dog scents and points
those dark, small-bodied pheasants which, when rousted, fly like
rockets to curl back into the reeds or land in the water. Point after
point, and the sheer pleasure of telling one's host that a bird lies in a
particular patch of reeds and will fly in seconds, is the epitome of the
relationship which can be created between handler and dog.

This is precision work, with none of the hit-and-miss of over-
exuberant spaniels or the plodding of retrievers. It is calculated,
clever dogwork, designed specifically to ensure that the gun gets the
chance of a fair shot and that every inch of ground is covered.

In the evening we flight the packs of wigeon as they whistle and
purr across the scudding clouds backlit by a half-moon. With half a
dozen down and retrieved, we call it a day and retire.

vii

INTRODUCTION

*　　*　　*

This book marks, I feel, a particular point in the development of the hunter-pointer-retriever, or HPR, breeds, as they are known in Britain today. In my view, gundogs in this country are at a crossroads. The dominance of the Labrador retriever and the English springer spaniel is under threat, due largely to the onset of disease and ill-considered backyard breeding. Both breeds have had a superb track record in the shooting field, but today there is a growing awareness amongst gundog handlers and owners that all is not well amongst these and several of our other native gundog breeds.

Disillusionment and unease have, in the last three decades, caused many owners who really work and shoot over their dogs to turn their attention to the HPRs. Led by the German short-haired pointer, the six breeds now used in Britain have a great deal to commend them, both in the field and on the bench. Derived from sound, disease-free Continental stock, the breeds have a variety of uses applicable to shooting, deerstalking and falconry in Britain; it is now becoming increasingly commonplace to see German short-haired pointers and to a lesser extent viszlas and German wire-haired pointers at work with the rough shooter or picker-up, or on the grouse moors where they are in their element.

The individual authors in this book are experts in their chosen breed and as such each has been given a brief to 'explain' his or her particular dog. No punches have been pulled, no text 'toned down' or altered.

The object of the book is to assist would-be HPR owners, or new owners, fully to understand and acquaint themselves with the dog of their choice and to understand the overall scene. In the past much nonsense has been written about these breeds by those who simply failed to appreciate their function. All, we were told, had mouths like rat traps and none would face water. Jealousy soon spreads half-truths and lies, but today competent, serious gundog owners and handlers readily acknowledge the fact that the HPRs can compete on level terms with the best of our native breeds.

These dogs, whatever their particular breeds, are going to play an important role in the shooting field over the next few years and they will become increasingly popular; herein lies the potential Achilles heel. Personally, I hope that they will never reach 'pet' or symbol status, for a popular image will go hand-in-glove with a deterioration in working ability, ignorant breeding, a decline in type and an increase in disease.

It is essential that the breed clubs and owners do not allow this to happen. They have only to look at the sad remnants of once-proud British working gundogs to note and learn the lesson.

THE ARRIVAL OF THE ALL-ROUNDERS

Colonel David Hancock MBE

THE HUNTER-POINTER-RETRIEVER

Britain has every reason to be proud of her contribution to the breeds of gundog in the world. Our sportsmen, supported by the landed families, developed the renowned breeds which are still active in the field today – pointers, setters and spaniels – although some of these breeds are sadly little used in the shooting field. If you want sheer style on the grouse moor, a dog which excels at flushing, starting or springing game, or a specialist retriever for efficient picking up, our sporting breeds are still supreme. But if you want a dog which is capable of hunting game, pointing out where it is and then retrieving to hand when it is shot, then you must choose a foreign breed.

It is, of course, absurd that British dog breeders, revered the world over, have not responded to the contemporary demand for all-round skills in a gundog. But the world of the pedigree dog, a twentieth-century phenomenon, makes it all but impossible to launch a new utility breed, despite the fact that our own pointer used to act as a retriever two centuries ago, as the paintings of George Morland and Ben Marshall illustrate. In my lifetime the quite astonishing prejudice against retrieving pointers has, paradoxically, led to our own pointer being eclipsed. I can recall over 30 years ago, that distinguished gundog writer Frank Warner Hill reviving the pointer-retriever concept in his column, only for one correspondent to reply with, 'Nothing spoils the manner and style of a young pointer or setter quicker than being allowed to retrieve . . . Every retrieving pointer I have seen had a mouth like a rat-trap.' Another, Mrs C. S. Darley of the well-known Watermill setters wrote, 'I well know that pointer and setter style is lost when you use one of these breeds for general purposes. These purposes must include hedge-hunting and that is the end of your setter setting and your pointer pointing.'

Against such entrenched views it is scarcely surprising that we have had to go abroad. Did our ancestors at the end of the eighteenth-century not prize style and seek soft-mouthed pointers which could retrieve? Rather puckishly, Warner Hill ended this controversial issue by quickly stating that the best gundog he ever saw on a grouse moor was a cross retriever-pointer, looking very much like a black pointer. It was owned by Tom Simpson when he was on Longshawe for the Duke of Devonshire.

Continental breeders have never hesitated to crossbreed or out-cross in the pursuit of excellence in the field. The great sporting dog fancier, Alban de Lamothe, once advised: 'The breeding of the wire-haired pointer and its enormous success in the field should be a lesson to those who regard the secondary and conventional characteristics as immutable dogma. They are in danger of forgetting that our hunting dogs belong to working breeds, not the category of domestic pets.' From that background and approach the HPR breeds came to us from Europe.

The working gundog scene in Britain has long been dominated by two breeds, the Labrador retriever and the English springer spaniel. Twenty years ago the Kennel Club registrations for gundog breeds were led by six breeds: Labrador retrievers (14,000), cocker spaniels (6,000), golden retrievers (5,000), Irish setters (2,600), English springer spaniels (2,500) and English setters (1,000). At that time our own pointer outnumbered the German short-haired pointer; the only other 'hunt, point and retrieve' breed was the Weimaraner and there were under 200 of them. Twenty years later the scene is very different.

Now the pointers from Germany (1,200 Weimaraners, 700 short-haired and 150 wire-haired) number well over three times as many as our own. We have in addition 70 Brittanies, 160 vizslas, 130 spinones and 60 large Münsterländers, proving the wide appeal of the Continental HPR breeds. In these circumstances, some of our older native breeds are struggling to survive, with fewer than 100 clumber, field and Sussex spaniels, only just over 100 curly-coated retrievers and some 150 Irish water spaniels. Human whim as well as merit plays its part in all of this, with some breeds being introduced by enterprising opportunists and others being discarded through mere fickleness. Before the middle of the last century, new gundogs imported from the Continent were sometimes a valuable infusion of new blood into our canine bloodstock. Now with the genepool closed in each of our pedigree breeds, new breeds arrive at the expense of our own breeds rather than enriching them.

DEVELOPMENT OF THE CONTINENTAL HUNTER-POINTER-RETRIEVER BREEDS

Pointing dogs have been known on the mainland of Europe for well over 700 years. Latini wrote in 1260 that, 'others are brachs with falling ears, which know of beasts and birds by their scent,' and Albertus Magnus recorded in 1280 that, 'they get to find the partridge by scent and thus ... they point ... at the ... birds'. One thousand years earlier, the Romans, too, made reference to a shaggy-haired dog called the Tuscan which would indicate unseen game, such a dog being of great value to hunters of any century, before and after the invention of firearms. In the sixteenth century Heresbach wrote that, 'Spanish dogs, zealous for their masters and of commendable sagacity, are chiefly used for finding partridges and hares.' Early in the seventeenth century, the naturalist Gesner noted that, 'We Germans and the French call these dogs quail-dogs ... the Italians call them net-dogs'. He referred to such dogs as 'vorstehhund', literally, dog that stands before.

In the eighteenth century, Tanzer was writing that, 'The best way to take partridges, as is done by princes and nobles, is to shoot the birds neatly, with a pointing dog; or take them by a pointing dog and nets. The sort of dog that is used is white and brown marked, or white and speckled.' At this time there were two distinct types of pointer in Spain: a hefty scent-hound type, believed to have been introduced from Italy in the thirteenth century, and the smaller, swifter type favoured in central Europe. In due course this latter type manifested itself in many different regions, as far apart as Weimar and Hungary, Poitou and Compiègne, Auvergne and Belgium. Setter-like dogs were favoured in Brittany, Picardy, Münster, Friesland and Drente. Coarse-haired pointing dogs were favoured in Piedmont, Lombardy, Hesse and Slovenia. In Hungary and Germany, pointing dogs were produced in smooth, coarse and long-haired varieties to give us the vizslas and the various German pointer types of today. According to Wenzel, the vizsla was known in the reign of the kings of the House of Arpad (eleventh to fourteenth centuries), but was used as an all-purpose hunting dog until the late nineteenth century. At that time the German pointer was being standardisèd through Hector I and Waldin, a whole-coloured brown dog. The Weimaraner, like the vizsla, was initially used as a multipurpose hunting dog, tracking deer and boar for example.

The coarse-haired dogs are collectively referred to as 'pointing griffons' and have a reputation for greater hardiness and determination. Some authorities believe that the Italian coarse-haired pointing griffon, the spinone, represents the most ancient form of this type of dog. Certainly the spinone was known throughout Piedmont,. in Venetia, Istria, Dalmatia and as far as the Danube, leading some to suppose the breed came from the east. The cynologist Tale records that a hundred years ago roan-coloured spinones were well known in Lombardy and Venetia, usually with longer and noticeably silkier, almost setter-like, hair. Another researcher, Tschudy, ascribes the origin of all pointing breeds to the Roman era, when Greek traders and others from the western Adriatic coast brought coarse-haired quail-dogs to be developed subsequently by sporting fanciers in what is now southern Italy.

The setting spaniel was known all over Europe in the Middle Ages, but then the words referred to what we now call setters or épagneuls. Of course our modern breeds of setter have developed in their own way throughout the last two or three centuries, but the setting dog is an established European type of sporting dog, evolving into separate breeds through local needs and preferences.

Espée de Selincourt, writing at the end of the seventeenth century and making early use of the generic term 'gundogs' (*chiens de l'arquebuse*), separated the spaniels from the braques. He defined setting dogs (*chiens couchants*) as 'braques that stop at the scent [*arrêtant tout*] and hunt with the nose high ... The spaniels are for the falcons [*oyseaux*], hunting with the nose low, and follow by the track.' But before the use of firearms in the field of hunting fur and feather, the net was the most common device: huge nets were drawn over both setting dog and the area containing the game being indicated. I am inclined to believe that the earliest sporting dogs other than hounds of the chase were the dogs *da rete* (of the net) and the water-dogs which would retrieve arrows and duck. The 'oysel' dogs of the sixteenth century were much more setter-like than anything else. It could be that the expression *chien d'arrêt* or stop-dog is a corruption of *da rete*.

A setting dog is featured in the 'Falconry' Tapestry, woven in the 1400s at Tournai. In 1563 Lord Warwick wrote to his brother, the Earl of Leicester, from Le Havre: 'I thank you for sending me so fine a horse. In return, I send you the best Setter in France ...' It is too limiting to think of setters in the British Isles developing from the land spaniel as a purely British-bred achievement. Sportsmen and women seek good dogs anywhere and everywhere; national boundaries have no relevance to them. Setters were depicted in paintings on the Continent long before they featured in paintings produced here. I do not believe that the Continental épagneul breeds have a separate origin from our setter breeds. All over Europe the setting breeds have long been favoured by the landed gentry and associated with the nobility; the higher-headed pointers and setters too have long been regarded as the aristocrats of the gundog world. But just as aristocratic families have interbred across national boundaries, so too have their dogs, including the setters, épagneuls and pointers of western Europe.

THE HUNTER-POINTER-RETRIEVER BREEDS IN BRITAIN

If you lined up a blue belton English setter with a large Münsterländer or a stabyhoun, a Brittany with a Welsh springer, a Drentse patrijshond with a black and white English setter, and a solid-coloured langhaar with an Irish setter, there are few observers who would not argue a common origin. I believe it is foolish and ill-informed to think of our setter breeds as coming purely from a land spaniel source, with the added blood of pointer, collie and hound, wholly in this country. The trading between Ireland and Spain, Wales and Brittany, London and Rotterdam, our south coast ports and their French counterparts over many centuries included valuable hunting dogs, however different their employment. Although the comparatively recent introduction of German pointers, Münsterländers, Brittanies and vizslas here as pedigree breeds is unusual for gundogs, I believe they are following a traditional route, disturbed for a century or so by our preference for specialist breeds in the shooting field. This preference, however, is now disappearing fast, with many sportsmen opting for German, French and Hungarian all-rounders, but not so far for the Dutch.

The shorter-haired, shortened-tailed HPR breeds are proving the most popular with British sportsmen and women, particularly German short-haired pointers, Weimaraners and vizslas. But Brittanies and German wire-haired pointers are now making ground too. The German short-haired pointer and the Brittany are finding favour with the rough-shooting fraternity.

The rough shooter expects his dog to range wide or close according to the terrain, confirmed by its handler's signals. It is expected to be a ground-scenter and an air-scenter, a soft-mouthed retriever and a gamefinder. It should be capable of holding game on point until its handler is within range and then flush; it must be able to work with equal ability in water, in dense cover or in open country. It is hardly surprising that a dog which has to adapt its range, head-height and pace, and then find, point and retrieve game, is open to criticism from purist pointer users. It is foolish to expect such a wide repertoire to be instilled easily or perfected effortlessly in a gundog. The all-rounders demand more time and more enlightened handling; they are *not* utility dogs for tyro-sportsmen but complex dogs for knowledgeable rough shooters.

These all-round Continental breeds have nevertheless made progress in spite of sustained opposition from some of the less far-seeing gundog writers, who have either ignored their usefulness or damned them with faint praise. I have nothing but admiration for these versatile dogs and I commend the pioneers who brought them to us. The HPR breeds are all doing well despite the peculiarity of English gamebirds and our fieldwork conditions. Having lived three times in Germany and worked extensively on the Continent, I know only too well how not just the terrain and cover but also the ways of sportsmen vary there. The adaptability of these breeds never ceases to amaze me. Who could not admire in any gundog breed the physical soundness of a Weimaraner like Ragstone Ritter, the sheer style of solid liver German short-haired pointer bitch Andesheim Utrice, the fine temperament of Major Wilkinson's black and white German wirehaired pointer bitch Vicky, imported from the Bocholter kennels, the desire to work of Angela Lewis's first British field trial champion Brittany, Riscoris Fleur de Lys, or the water prowess of Di Arrowsmith's first British field champion Weimaraner, Wobrooke of Fleetapple?

The large Münsterländer may not work as fast or cover the same amount of ground as a German short-haired pointer, but it is good in water, will work moorland and stubble like a pointer, and yet will take on dense cover like a spaniel. In flatter ground Münsterländers have been accused of getting too close to their birds and flushing them prematurely. But the breed was given an excellent start over here through the importation in 1972 of three unrelated bitches from the best blood lines in Germany. Eight years ago I was impressed by the steadiness of Mrs Jean Beddow's bitch, Datroy Ingaveld, and the temperament of two other bitches, Doranburg Ariadne and Doranburg Aspiration. I find this breed the most affectionate of the HPRs.

The small Münsterländer, or Westphalian setter, stands just over 20 inches at the shoulder and is around 50 lbs in weight. Brown and white or brown roan and often heavily flecked, this breed is much more like the Brittany than its bigger relatives. Developed a hundred years ago from the old long-haired pointing breeds and heath-quail dogs, the spaniel blood sometimes gets the better of the setter instincts, but I would recommend them for their stamina, robustness and temperament. The latter is so often given a foolishly low priority in gundog breeds.

Some years back a vizsla, Angela Saunders's Jaridon Wicked Witch, was most impressive when gaining her title in obedience work. I admired too the conformation of the Russetmantle dogs and the steadfastness of the Gardenway bitches I saw. The vizsla bitch, Swallow Skylark, owned and handled by Mrs P.J. Easy, has earned good ratings at pointing tests on grouse, looking every inch a 'golden hunting dog'. There is no loss of type in this breed; how I would like to be able to say that of our springers!

The lesser-known breeds from the Continent, Dutch breeds like the stabyhoun and the Drentse patrijshond, French breeds like the korthals griffon, Italian breeds like the spinone and the bracco, and the hertha pointer of Denmark, are not appreciated in the British Isles, although the spinone has very recently become established. Their lack of popularity, however, has left them largely unspoiled, free of physical and mental inherited diseases and not bred too 'hot' for the average rough shooter, seeking a companion as well as a gundog. The spinone could be one of the oldest breeds utilised to indicate unseen game, a modern representative of an ancient proto-type.

The stabyhoun comes from the province of Friesland and is related to the Drentse patrijshond, already known in this country. Rather like a small Landseer Newfoundland, the stabyhoun is a most versatile working dog for rough shooting: fast and determined, yet steady, obedient, robust and able to last a hard day without showing undue fatigue. It reminds me very much of the late Dr J.B. Maurice's outstanding English setters which, bearing the 'Downsman' prefix, so distinguished themselves at field trials some 30 years ago. These Dutch setters, only a foot and a half at the shoulder, are in essence unsophisticated all-rounders, but they give a bold, quick-thinking and unflappable performance, and deserve greater acclaim. Little known and unspoiled, they represent a sound traditional breed of which only the best were used for breeding, so that today we have an intelligent, eager, tireless dog, affectionate but never fawning, alert but never neurotic, a faithful companion yet a highly efficient working breed.

The Drentse patrijshond – the partridge dog from the province of Drente – is a bigger breed, usually with more white colouring but otherwise quite similar to the stabyhoun, to which it is also related. If you visit the Rjiksmuseum in Amsterdam and study Dutch paintings of two centuries ago, you will find sporting dogs of those times depicted just as the patrijshond is today. Unlike the other Dutch sporting breeds, this one is recognised by our Kennel Club as a pedigree breed but has never become established here.

The hertha pointer achieved its name from the founding dam of the breed, which may have come from the kennel of the Duke of Augustenborg on the island of Als, off southern Jutland. She was found wandering with soldiers of the defeated Danish army in the war with Germany in 1864. She was of the particular coat colouring which the Duke favoured, rather as in Britain the Duke of Kingston preferred black pointers in the eighteenth century. Hertha, later called Old Hertha, became a famous hunting dog in the forests of Jutland and was mated with a chestnut-red pointer from the Duke's stock to found this canine dynasty. It might have been better to have retained the name 'hertha-hound', but many Danish sportsmen outcrossed to English pointers and today we have the hertha pointer. Hertha pointer blood is a vital ingredient in every English pointer bred in Denmark. It is likely, however, that the old hertha-hound was an all-round hunting dog of some distinction, and those devotees in Denmark who want to restore the breed as such are probably on the right lines.

I suspect that this yellow-orange Danish pointer is connected with the ancestors of other European sporting breeds like the Weimaraner in southern Germany and the vizsla of Hungary. They are all distinctively marked, self-coloured hunting dogs with a hound look about them. Such dogs were used all over central Europe in the sixteenth century to hunt quail with nets, and some cynologists link their origin with the yellow Turkish quail-hunting dog.

Further south in Europe we have the bracco italiano and the spinone. It is easy to spot the hound links in these two Italian breeds, with their throatiness and turned ears. I have never seen the bracco italiano working but the spinone is impressive and keen, thorough yet not too highly charged. Some authorities connect orange and white pointers with the old Piedmont spaniel and the roan with Lombardy. Experts like Tschudy claim that the setting breeds originated in north Italy in Roman times, whilst Tale links the roan spinone with the silkier-haired dogs of Lombardy and Venetia. I doubt if British sportsmen will go for these Italian dogs, but I am surprised that the German long-haired pointer has not found favour.

The langhaar is a good-looker and a worker, racier than the Dutch setters, strong-limbed, powerful and eager. Solid brown or parti-coloured, just over 2 feet at the withers, long-haired, with a full tail or one slightly 'rounded', it is related to the épagneul breeds and the German wachtelhund or spaniel, the latter being the German 'stöberhund' or flushing dog. It has the short, high (French) ear but undoubtedly the blood of our own setters has been introduced. Tall, elegant and upstanding, the langhaar is for me the best-looking German gundog.

Not especially handsome but a superb worker, the korthals griffon is hardly known here. If you were to ask me to choose an HPR on

FT Ch. Riscoris Fleur de Lys and Sugarloaf Chasseur of Dorvalstan,
Brittanies owned by Mrs A. Lewis and
Mr W. C. Stanley-Smith respectively

Sh. Ch. Midwill Zac and Shalina Ballerina,
Weimaraners owned by Mrs P. Cuttings and Mrs P. Bradley

Tudor Carol of Austringer and Austringer Wey of Stockhill,
GSPs owned by Mr and Mrs R. Kuban

Phizers Fugelman, a GSP owned by Mrs D. Mendoza

purely field use, I would go for a korthals griffon. Created by a master breeder, developed in a stern school, unspoilt and expected to excel, this coarse-haired griffon has a real edge to its performance.

LOOKING TO THE FUTURE

If, in the middle of the last century, British sportsmen and women had found the need for an all-round gundog, able to hunt, point and retrieve, they would have bred one themselves and it would have been a world-beater. Now we mainly capitalise on sound German breeding whilst our own pointer, which originally retrieved too, is restricted to its specialist use. In a hundred years' time, we may well come to regret this intransigence. For I can see these Continental all-rounders going from strength to strength in Britain.

Over the next decade I can see the German short-haired pointer, the Weimaraner and the vizsla steadily increasing their numbers, with HPR working tests and field trials in time outnumbering the others. Two breeds I see really making ground are the German wire-haired pointer and the Brittany, and I would not be at all surprised to see a thousand of each being registered here by the end of the century. I would like to see the korthals griffon and the small Münsterländer taken up by an enlightened patron; both breeds are great workers and have so much to offer the rough shooter. Let no one be mistaken, the HPR breeds are not only here to stay but are going to disturb our contemporary preference for specialist breeds and functions in no uncertain terms. But if we are to make best use of their all-round performance, it is absolutely vital for British sportsmen and women to accept that they are different; they pose a bigger challenge to the trainer and it is simply foolish to regard them as a more versatile springer or a setter with an extended role.

It would be a great pity if the distinctive Weimaraner and the handsome vizsla were to become mainly show dogs, although their considerable cosmetic appeal is undeniable, and for the superb working abilities of the Brittany to be prejudiced by well-intentioned but unenlightened novice owner-handlers. These Continental all-rounders are essentially working dogs, working in a different style, a style strange to most of our sportsmen and women. Happily there are signs that the breed clubs concerned are both knowledgeable and true to the heritage of their breeds. For without dedicated support and informed awareness of the breed characteristics involved in these gifted dogs, we could end up spoiling fine breeds developed by master breeders in pursuit of field performance. Many of our native sporting breeds sadly illustrate only too clearly the way in which two hundred years of inspired breeding can be destroyed in two decades of certificate chasing.

My plea therefore is to the breeders and the trainers of HPR breeds. We must breed for the best and from the best, and never merely in pursuit of show-ring conformation. We must retain the sheer versatility of these talented dogs and keep faith with the Continental devotees who dedicated their whole lives to the correct development of their particular breeds. But even the best bred gundogs need gifted trainers. The HPR breeds show early signs of instinctive behaviour yet mature slowly. A German short-haired pointer at one year is very different from, say, a Labrador of that age. Professional trainers are therefore given less scope and this could result in capable amateur owner-handlers, able and willing to devote more time to their own dogs, excelling with HPR breeds.

This slow maturity must never be confused with stupidity or lack of innate ability. Here is a group of dogs that can follow wounded game or track deer and boar, work with the falcon, quarter ground close or wide, hold game on point, flush on command, mark and retrieve shot game, work in water and dense cover, withstand the cold and wet, and yet provide companionable loyalty and affection for their owners. Theirs is a rich heritage and one we must honour. With the arrival of the all-rounders, the British gundog scene is changing fast, and both trainers and fieldwork organisers are faced with a new but exciting challenge.

2

THE
BRITTANY

Angie Lewis

The first thing to establish about the Brittany is that, despite appearances, it is *not* a spaniel. It is not even a pointing spaniel. Brittanies belong most definitely to the HPR group and, to avoid confusion, the Kennel Club dropped the word 'spaniel' from the original name within two years of the formation of the national breed club, at its members' request. The Irish still retain the old name and in France, the country of origin, it is known as the épagneul Breton.

ORIGINS AND HISTORY

There is much speculation on the origin of the breed, bringing with it a 'chicken and egg' syndrome when reference is made to the similarity of Brittanies to Welsh springers. Which came first? At first glance there is a resemblance between the two breeds but when side by side the heavier build of the Welsh makes the Brittany look light in bone. In temperament the two breeds differ as the Welsh seems quite sensible and placid compared to the Brittany's exuberance and joy of life. Both breeds, however, display a marked single-minded tenacity when it comes to finding game and both will stick to a line like glue when on runners, even through live unshot game. Add to this the

Breed standard

General appearance   Workmanlike, compact, lively, squarely built.

Characteristics   Energetic, intelligent, HPR.

Temperament   Affectionate and eager to please.

Head and skull   Medium length, rounded with the median line slightly visible. Stop well defined but not too deep. Occiput not pronounced but can be felt. Muzzle about two-thirds the length of the skull, tapered but not snipy. Nostrils open and well shaped.

Eyes   Expressive, brown to dark hazel, never light or hard in expression. Well set in.

Ears   Drop ears, set high, rather short, lightly fringed and vine shaped, covered with straight hair.

Mouth   Jaws strong with a perfect regular scissor bite, i.e. upper teeth closely overlapping the lower teeth and set square to the jaws. Lips tight, upper lip slightly overlapping lower.

Neck   Medium length, clean and well set on.

Forequarters   Sloping and well set on shoulders. Forelegs straight with good muscle. Moderately well boned. Feathered.

Body   Chest deep, descending to the level of elbow. Ribs well rounded. Back short with loin short and strong with slight slope of croup to hindquarters.

Hindquarters   Strong and broad, flanks well rounded, stifles well bent. Hocks well let down. Feathered to mid-thigh.

Feet   Small, compact with a little hair between toes.

Gait/movement   Straight and true.

Tail   Naturally short or customarily docked to 10 cm (4 inches) with a small twist of hair on the end. Carried level with back.

Coat   Body coat rather flat, dense, fairly fine and slightly wavy.

Colour   Orange/white, liver/white, black/white or roan or any of these colours or tri-colour. Nose dark in harmony with coat colour.

Size   Height maximum 51 cms.
Ideal height: dogs 48–50 cm (19–20 in.); bitches 47–49 cm (18–19 in.)
Ideal weight: dogs 15 kgs (33 lbs); bitches 13 kgs (28½ lbs).

Faults   Any departure from the foregoing points should be considered a fault and the seriousness with which the fault should be regarded should be in exact proportion to its degree.

Note   Male animals should have two apparently normal testicles fully descended into the scrotum.

colouring of red and white, and the close affinity between Wales and Brittany through the ages, and perhaps the two breeds are branches of the same tree.

The short tail is an important feature, however, so where does that come from? It has been suggested that the Italian bracco and the braque de Bourbonnais, both pointing breeds, the latter also having a short tail, went into the French spaniel's breeding, so giving us a base from which to start. It is generally agreed that both spaniel and setter blood are behind the modern Brittany.

As far as we know the breed officially originated in the Callac area of Brittany, known there as 'le fougères', the high-spirited one. It is known that the English aristocracy regularly visited France to shoot woodcock and other game in the last century, taking their pointers and setters with them. For convenience the setters were left over there in the off season so it is likely that a bit of crossing went on with the local spaniels, gradually finishing with a short-tailed pointing/retrieving dog which suited the local terrain. Enthusiasts joined together in 1907 and formed the first breed club.

Although a few Brittanies came to Great Britain with American servicemen or *en route* to other countries, none were registered with the Kennel Club so no contribution was made to the breed. Things started to happen in 1981 when four of French breeding were imported to Eire and then Mr Stanley Smith of Kent brought in his foundation stock of a dog and bitch. The Irish dogs were Phebus de Saint Lubin, son of international beauty and field trial champion, Nat du Buison de Choisel; a black and white bitch, Perlez de Kerryvann; an orange and white dog, Tr. Orius de Saint Tugen, which died in an accident and was replaced by an orange and white dog, Serry de Sous les Viviers; and an orange and white bitch, Roez de Saint Tugen. There is now an active breed club in existence in Ireland.

Meanwhile in England Stan Smith was making the breed more available by mating his first imports, Puk des Pigenettes, an orange and white dog, and Rolline de Saint Tugen, an orange and white roan bitch. A bitch from this litter was later mated to Ted de Sous Les Viviers, which produced the breed's first field trial champion, Riscoris Fleur de Lys.

Another import of Stan's was Samantha de Goas Vilinic, which he mated back to Puk. This litter produced the breed's first field trial award winner in Dorvalstan Ulrick of Riscoris. Ulrick won two novice stakes in his first season, then went on to win an open non-qualifier and some all-aged stakes before qualifying for the HPR championships by winning a second in an open qualifier. Unfortunately, due to back injury he was unable to compete and had to be retired from competition. Ulrick sired two field triallers when mated to a bitch which was half American breeding and half French. His brother,

Dorvalstan Umberto, also did well in trials; both these dogs were very easy to train and a pleasure to handle.

Initially there was a lot of discussion on whether to mix American and French breeding, as the two types are rather different. With such a small genepool a couple of breeders have gone ahead and the results have been encouraging from a working point of view, one bitch, Victoria of Talwater, gaining a second in an open qualifier to run in the 1988 championship, where she gained a diploma of merit. The two litter sisters by Dorvalstan Ulrick also descend from 'mixed blood', namely Bredebeck Blanche and Belle, which are presently in open competition having won a novice stake each plus other awards. Another bitch, Raffia Run of Presthill, has also won minor trial awards, sired by Ted out of an American bitch.

Field trial champion Riscoris Fleur de Lys started her career more slowly, winning seconds and thirds at first but gaining a first at the Hampshire Gundog Society novice stake in December 1985. In 1986 she won her way out of novice stakes by winning the Weimaraner Club's novice at Capel. In 1987 she started her first season in open competition. Again she took her time, getting seconds and thirds in all-aged stakes, but just before Christmas she pulled off the first open qualifier at Woodhall Park. In the New Year she won an all-aged stake then had another third, but she was saving it all for the last day of the season and the open qualifier at Marston in Oxfordshire, run again by the Weimaraner Club.

Another significant importer is Ray Greenwood of Wales, who was responsible for bringing in the black and white and liver and white dogs, namely Urak of Joymonds and Unter de Saige Foemanoir respectively. Uhelenn de Saint Lubin, an orange and white bitch, is settled at this kennel along with the liver and white bitch Urka Du Pin Purdo, and litter brother and sister But de Saint Lubin and Croquette de Saint Lubin, both orange and white. Although Ray admits that he is not able to work his dogs for lack of time, he is very keen to keep the working ability alive and has them trained to this end. Messrs Green and Gorman have recently imported tricolours which add to the few that have now been bred in this country. Thanks to these few pioneers, we are gradually increasing in numbers and, one hopes, in fans.

Crufts 1984 saw a meeting of interested parties form the Brittany Spaniel Club of Great Britain. By September 1985 the club was registered by the Kennel Club but with one very significant change: the word 'Spaniel' was dropped from the name to avoid confusion and criticism from other groups of gundog enthusiasts. Since that first meeting the club has gone from strength to strength, running working tests, training days, an open show and pointing tests, while in 1989 its first novice field trial will take place. In America the breed is extremely popular, with many dual champions and field champions, their breed club having been in existence since 1942. The 'American' type is slightly different to the French, bigger all over, displaying mainly pink noses, lighter eyes and eye-rims, and longer muzzles.

BREED CHARACTERISTICS AND TEMPERAMENT

Brittanies come in a variety of colours. The most popular is orange and white, when the orange can range from light orange to dark mahogany. Liver and white, black and white and tricolour make up the range, and any of these colours can appear as roan or clear colour. In America any black is taboo, in the coat, on eye-rims or nose, although the British Kennel Club accepts any of these colours.

The shape of a Brittany is very different to that of Britain's indigenous spaniels as it has a short back and longish legs, giving the impression of a square dog in outline. The head is quite small and neat, but do not be misled by the apparent smallness of the mouth into thinking that the breed cannot cope with large game. Brittanies are similar to cockers in this respect and will, with experience, hold cock pheasants and hares quite comfortably. The tail is normally docked very short to balance the short back, although some puppies are born tailless.

Brittanies on point seem to look much bigger than when they are relaxed as they stretch the neck with the intensity of the point and rise up on the toes. They are able to cope with all types of ground including moorland, whilst thick cover is barged at to push a bird out and they will tackle nettles and thistles happily, helped by their thick coats. I have also found the coat to dry quickly after water work, and the skin is not even wet after a swim. Another plus is that, being a bit taller on the leg than a spaniel, their stomachs do not get so muddy, and as the coat is of a silky texture it sheds debris quickly. The ears are small and set high on the head, which gives the alert look and also does away with the ear troubles to which spaniels are prone. The eyes are set well in the head and are therefore not easily damaged; nor do they show the haw and collect rubbish.

The character of the Brittany is complex and contradictory. The only thing it has in common with the spaniel is its love of hunting. Actually, Brittanies have a passion for hunting, which might explain their initial indifference to retrieving, but more of that later. A good Brittany covers the ground at great speed, head up, sometimes whipping round on point, or leaping in the air as it catches a whiff of game and landing on point. This makes for a very exciting dog to watch at work, but can be a bit disconcerting if you are not used to a fast dog working out of shot. However, in wooded country Brittanies seem to know it is more sensible to stay closer to the gun; indeed they have an endearing habit of coming back to check on your where-abouts, usually with an impatient expression!

Off duty they can have an excitable, high-spirited temperament and are friendly, although some have a reserve and take their time to accept strangers. The whole stance of a Brittany should convey an alertness and interest in everything about them, but do not confuse eagerness with wildness when working. They can, and do, settle down to become sensible, reliable shooting companions with consistent training.

REARING AND TRAINING

I would emphasise that early training in manners is essential to retain that willingness to please displayed by most puppies. A Brittany that is allowed to hunt for itself will become a strong-willed hooligan by 1 year old if it is a bold type, but be careful not to overdo heavy heel work or your pup may not leave your heels at all.

I have found them to be a breed which benefits from hunting on different terrain to make them familiar with natural obstacles; they seem to be slower than other breeds at accepting fences, hedges, etc. but, once mastered, they are often very courageous, reckless even. The same attitude applies to water work. It may take months to get them to accept it, but once confidence is there they will have a go at anything.

When Brittanies were introduced into this country much was made of the 'iron hand in the velvet glove' approach to training them. The word 'sensitive' was also much used. However, I have found Brittanies to be pretty tough cookies and, as far as retrieving is concerned, I now adopt a policy of teaching the retrieve just as I would any other exercise. Some will not take this approach and become sweet pets but, as an HPR breed, retrieving is obviously just one part of the job. I have found that once taught they become very efficient retrievers but with some dogs much perseverance is necessary. As with all breeds you get the so-called 'naturals' which need little persuasion to pick up, but do not make the mistake of thinking that because your young Brittany carries objects around the house, or even brings you 'presents', that it is a 'natural'! When it comes to putting on some pressure and getting them to retrieve in the field, all such previous willingness evaporates, leaving you with a sulky wimp, or so they would have you believe. It is at this point that I believe many Brittanies will be discarded as non-retrievers, particularly by trainers of other breeds who may misunderstand the breed.

Do not be dismayed if a young Brittany hardly looks at you at all! This type is usually a cracking hunter, pure hell to train but well worth the effort. It is hard to put aside preconceived ideas; one of mine was 'I cannot train a dog that won't look at me', but I have learnt that all is not as it seems. Brittanies can lead you a merry dance in their training period, particularly over dummies, which is why they are generally not good working-test dogs, but do not discard that stubborn, arrogant little toad – you may well be very pleasantly surprised when it comes to the real thing.

However, do not rush or skip the 'squarebashing', as the enthusiasm for hunting can easily take over and leave you with a non-retrieving hunting machine with very defective brakes! Actually, I have found that those which sat and gazed at me as puppies turned out to be very sensitive and unable to take any pressure when introduced to commands rather than requests. This is part of the contradictory character of the Brittany to which I referred earlier.

How do you explain that they will, on the one hand, take discipline if they know they are defying you and deserve it, and yet, on the other, collapse in a heap if asked to do a simple dummy retrieve, turning the head away with a dramatic flourish and refusing to watch you throw the darn thing? Is it worth all this hassle? You can try them on cold game and they respond for a while, but basically they just really want to hunt. Maybe I am a masochist but, yes, it is worth it because when it all comes right and you discover they have absorbed much more of the boring stuff than you ever thought possible, that is a very sweet moment. To watch a Brittany working with vigour, after a long, gruelling hunt, avidly watching where that bird came down, every muscle strained and waiting for your permission to collect that elusive cock pheasant, makes it all worthwhile.

I have probably given the impression that all Brittanies are extremely hard work and virtually untrainable by the average shooting man or woman, but I must admit that there are a few specimens that almost train themselves and these are a joy for anyone to own. I am trying to give an overall picture of the breed as it is in Great Britain at present, culled from those I have seen and trained.

The one aspect of a Brittany which I would describe as 'sensitive' is the pointing/steadiness part. If a young Brittany points and then goes slowly forward without a command and flushes the game it is very easy to put the pup off pointing by being too heavy on the discipline. They can sometimes get confused and not point at all, or will sit immediately at the point. Similarly, if the pup rushes in to flush and chases, be careful not to be too hard. This is one area that I leave well alone and simply give the dog time to learn to hold its point. Give them time and practise stopping on the whistle in retrieving exercises, or general obedience away from game. Do not be frightened by the speed of the dog or panic if it seems to be miles from you; build up the relationship between you with training and you will find that a Brittany wants to be with you.

The only certain conclusion I have come to since owning Brittanies is that they are unlike anything else! The Continental trainers of Brittanies, who of course have many more years of experience of the breed than me, advise that they do not worry about the retrieving; 'leave them alone and they will come to it' is their retort. Perhaps in future years we can breed for a more casual approach to this side of the dogs' ability.

So there you have it, a fascinating addition to the HPR group, with a fluid short gait, enormous stamina, very strong neck and shoulders, an ability to lift game sometimes bigger than themselves, and a short tail to avoid injury and vets' bills. If you are unlucky enough to get a sticky retriever all you have to do is decide which course to take, either hope the penny drops when you get on to game, as it frequently does, or persist with the dummy training. This little dog has had a very good start in field trials in its early years in Britain, so all that remains is to hope that it gains in popularity in the shooting field. Many Brittanies are also filling the role of the falconer's dog with success, making it a versatile animal well worth your attention.

3

THE GERMAN SHORT-HAIRED POINTER

Richard and Sheila Kuban

ORIGINS AND HISTORY

A dog for all seasons – this was the aim of those who set about developing the German short-haired pointer. The demand for such a dog came in the latter half of the nineteenth century from the less wealthy sportsmen who wanted what we now call a rough-shooting dog; one which would be an integral part of a hunting team; a dog which would get out and find game which was scarce, over any type of terrain, would point staunchly until its handler was in a position to shoot, and would retrieve from land and water. They also wanted the dog to be able to track wounded animals and, if necessary, to kill those which counted as predators. On top of all this the dog was also to be good-looking!

Needless to say there was a good deal of disagreement between those engaged in the formation of this multipurpose breed as to what mixture of the types of dog available at that time should be used. It is generally accepted that, to produce the pointing virtues, the breed known as the Old Spanish pointer played a major part and in the early experiments this was mixed with indigenous hunting dogs of hound background. Other breeds were probably added as each experimenter pursued his particular line of thought on how the ultimate dog should

Breed standard

General appearance Noble, steady dog showing power, endurance and speed, giving the immediate impression of an alert and energetic dog whose movements are well co-ordinated. Of medium size, with a short back standing over plenty of ground. Grace of outline, clean-cut head, long sloping shoulders, deep chest, short back, powerful hindquarters, good bone composition, adequate muscle, well-carried tail and taut coat.

Characteristics Dual purpose pointer-retriever, very keen nose, perseverance in searching and initiative in game finding, excellence in field, a naturally keen worker, equally good on land and water.

Temperament Gentle, affectionate and even-tempered. Alert, biddable and very loyal.

Head and skull Clean cut, neither too light nor too heavy, well proportioned to body. Skull sufficiently broad and slightly round. Nasal bone rising gradually from nose to forehead (this more pronounced in dogs) and never possessing a definite stop, but when viewed from side a well-defined stop effect due to position of eyebrows. Lips falling away almost vertically from somewhat protruding nose and continuing in a slight curve to corner of mouth. Lips well developed, not over hung. Jaws powerful and sufficiently long to enable the dog to pick up and carry game. Dish-faced and snipey muzzle undesirable. Nose solid brown or black depending on coat colour. Wide nostrils, well-opened and soft.

Eyes Medium size, soft and intelligent, neither protruding nor too deep set. Varying in shades of brown to tone with coat. Light eye undesirable. Eyelids should close properly.

Ears Broad and set high; neither too fleshy nor too thin, with a short, soft coat; hung close to head, no pronounced fold, rounded at tip and reaching almost to corner of mouth when brought forward.

Mouth Teeth sound and strong. Jaws strong, with a perfect, regular and complete scissor bite, i.e. upper teeth closely overlapping lower teeth and set square to the jaws.

Neck Moderately long, muscular and slightly arched, thickening towards shoulders. Skin not fitting too loosely.

Forequarters Shoulders sloping and very muscular, top of shoulder blades close; upper arm bones, between shoulder and elbow, long. Elbows well laid back, neither pointing outwards nor inwards. Forelegs straight and lean, sufficiently muscular and strong, but not coarse-boned. Pasterns slightly sloping.

Body Chest must appear deep rather than wide but in proportion to rest of body; ribs deep and well sprung, never barrel-shaped or flat; back ribs reaching well down to tuck up of loins. Chest measurement immediately behind elbows smaller than about a hand's breadth behind elbows, so that upper arm has freedom of movement. Firm, short back, not arched. Loin wide and slightly arched; croup wide and sufficiently long, neither too heavy nor too sloping, starting on a level with back and sloping gradually towards tail. Bones solid and strong. Skin should not fit loosely or fold.

Hindquarters Hips broad and wide, falling slightly towards tail. Thighs strong and well muscled. Stifles well bent. Hocks square with body and slightly bent, turning neither in nor out. Pasterns nearly upright.

Feet Compact, close-knit, round to spoon shaped, well padded, turning neither in nor out. Toes well arched with strong nails.

Tail Starts high and thick growing gradually thinner, customarily docked to medium length by two-fifths to half its length. When quiet, tail carried down, when moving, horizontally; never held high over back or bent.

Gait/movement Smooth lithe gait essential. As gait increases from walk to a faster speed, legs converge beneath body (single tracking). Forelegs reach well ahead, effortlessly covering plenty of ground with each stride and followed by hindlegs, which give forceful propulsion.

Coat Short, flat and coarse to touch, slightly longer under tail.

Colour Solid liver, liver and white spotted, liver and white spotted and ticked, liver and white ticked, solid black or black and white same variations (not tricolour).

Size Dogs minimum height at 58 cm (23 in.) at withers, maximum height 64 cm (25 in.) at withers. Bitches minimum height 53 cm (21 in.) at withers, maximum height 59 cm (23 in.) at withers.

Faults Any departure from the foregoing points should be considered a fault and the seriousness with which the fault should be regarded should be in exact proportion to its degree.

Note Male animals should have two apparently normal testicles fully descended into the scrotum.

---

look and perform, and from early illustrations of the breed in these formative years it would seem that some very odd specimens emerged. However, by the end of the nineteenth century some conformity of type and behaviour had appeared, and to improve the most important requirement of the breed, good scenting ability, many breeders were introducing blood from the pointer, the thoroughbred of pointing dogs, developed in England.

It took about 30 years to mould and form this utility breed, and when it had become well established it was apparent that its creators had produced a dog which was not only well able to fill their requirements in the hunting field but also aesthetically pleasing, free from any exaggerated features of conformation and with a character possessed of a real *joi de vivre*. The happy disposition of the German short-haired pointer is a particularly endearing feature, and the fact that it can work with energy and enthusiasm in the shooting field yet in the home be a family dog is a bonus.

The German short-haired pointer is undoubtedly the most popular of all the HPR breeds as far as British sportsmen and women are concerned. Although there were probably a few specimens in this country after its acceptance as a breed in Germany, the breed was officially introduced to Britain in the late 1940s, when dogs were brought back by members of the armed forces returning after the war. These owners had obviously been very impressed by the versatility of the German dogs and had no doubt acquired a taste for rough shooting in Germany, where game was sparse and the skill and combined efforts of man and dog in hunting were of more importance than the actual bag at the end of the day. They saw a niche for the breed in this country at a time when some of the very large estates were being broken up and shooting was becoming less formal. However, there was reluctance on the part of the devotees of the established gundog breeds to accept a dog which could both point *and* retrieve. Indeed, the Kennel Club found it difficult for some time to find a place in their field trial schedules for such a breed. In the early days of the breed in Britain, German short-haired pointers ran in pointer and setter trials with some success and it was not until 1958, following much hard work by the early enthusiasts and the formation of a breed club, that the Kennel Club made allowance in its Field Trial Rules and Regulations to cover breeds which hunt, point and retrieve.

Once given Kennel Club recognition, both in the show ring and for field trials, several champions were made up and some prominent strains began to emerge based on the original German imports. It is to the credit of the early enthusiasts of the breed in this country that they were insistent that breed type should not become split between the show dogs and those which worked. To this day it is the aim of the breed clubs to avoid any divergence in type. The measure of their success is the fact that over the last six years no fewer than five dual champions have been crowned, dogs which have achieved the titles of both show champion and field trial champion, a feat virtually unheard of in any other gundog breed since the war.

Since the early days of the German short-haired pointer in Britain, other imports have been introduced from the Continent and also the USA, and enthusiasm has grown for the breed in both the show ring and the shooting field. Of course, the followers of the more established gundog breeds are still inclined to use the 'jack of all trades' label when assessing the working ability of the German short-haired pointer, but its devotees view the breed more as a canine triathlete. Inevitably, individual dogs will become better at some aspects of work than others according to the environment they are brought up in, but with such a diversity of function the chances of a dog being a complete failure at everything are less likely.

BREED CHARACTERISTICS AND TEMPERAMENT

When contemplating the purchase of a gundog for work one must first determine what type of work the dog will be expected to perform. For obvious reasons, if driven shooting is to be the sole pursuit then the hunting and pointing abilities of this breed are superfluous. German short-haired pointers made to wait at a peg all day usually become thoroughly frustrated and bored, tending to fidget and squeak. Many German short-haired pointers become very useful dogs for wildfowling, being bold and purposeful when retrieving from water and marshland. However, their thin coat puts them at a disadvantage over retriever breeds in coping with extremes of cold if used exclusively for wildfowling. It also has to be remembered that the German short-haired pointer at its best is a fast, wide-ranging dog and some people are mentally and physically unable to cope with a dog which works beyond the range of the gun, no matter how staunch a pointer it might be. It would seem that the majority of gundog owners who find that the breed meets their needs are those whose sport is quite varied, mainly consisting of rough and walked-up shooting over a variety of terrain, wildfowling now and then and with perhaps the occasional trip to the grouse moors. Such owners derive great pleasure from the fact that they can take their dogs anywhere, and indeed there are some who add deerstalking and falconry to their programme of work.

Having decided that a German short-haired pointer would meet all the requirements of one's sporting activities, consideration must be given as to whether the particular characteristics of this breed of dog can be handled within one's own everyday circumstances. German short-haired pointers take very well to being part of a family environment and being included in its activities. In fact they will share your bed if allowed to! However, their role as fast ground-covering workers manifests itself in puppies and youngsters in boisterous playfulness, which the very young or elderly may find it difficult to cope with. In addition, boredom can develop into destructive and sometimes noisy behaviour. If this is going to be a problem then the provision of a kennel and run is essential.

Another consideration is the amount of ground to which the dog should be allowed unsupervised access. It is not uncommon for people enquiring about owning a German short-haired pointer to say, when told that they require a fair amount of exercise, that this will not be a problem because the dog will have six acres of garden in which to run to its heart's content! This is a sure recipe for creating an unmanageable dog. The hunting instinct is very strong in the German short-haired pointer, and a dog which has learned to hunt on its own will always do so. Again such a home environment calls for a kennel and run. Furthermore, on the question of daily exercise there is a misapprehension that because an adult German short-haired pointer is physically capable of coping with a 10-mile run every day it is necessary to give it this much exercise. The fitter the dog becomes, the more difficult it will be to satisfy its energy. Obviously a dog expected to work all day and every day on the moor has to be supremely fit, but the majority of dogs perhaps being worked two or three days a week rough shooting during the season can manage to keep sufficiently fit on two regular half-hour runs off the lead per day.

REARING AND TRAINING

To be of any use a fast, wide-ranging dog with a greater diversity of function than any other must enjoy a good relationship with its handler. It is therefore extremely important that much care is taken in fostering this relationship right from the time the puppy leaves the nest. Studies in dog behaviour have determined that from eight weeks puppies kept together form their social position within the pack and their particular characteristics are determined for life, whether they will be bold or timid and how they will meet and cope with problems presented to them. It follows, therefore, that a puppy introduced to its new home just before this time stands a better chance of being moulded into the ways of its new pack leader than if left until later. This is not to say that a puppy purchased at an older age cannot develop into a dog of balanced character and good working ability. There are many cases of trainers making second- or even third-hand dogs into useful working companions and even gaining working-test and field trial awards with them. But these dogs would undoubtedly have been even better had they started life with their successful owner. It is important when purchasing a puppy of ten weeks onwards to ascertain that it has been given plenty of human contact up to that time. German short-haired pointers enjoy human company and involvement but their boldness and vigour belies an under-lying sensitivity. Lack of human contact in these character-forming months can result in a consequent lack of confidence and in training difficulties.

There is seldom any difficulty in introducing a German short-haired pointer puppy into a home where there is already a dog or dogs. They mix well with other dogs and, in fact, usually settle down with their older companions as if they were foster parents. In these circumstances the usual problems associated with young puppies planted in unfamiliar surroundings, such as noisiness at night, are usually avoided. It might be as well to mention here that care should be taken if the puppy's new companions are very elderly or physically delicate. Boisterous German short-haired pointer puppies do not recognise these characteristics! Puppies being introduced to a dogless home usually need a lot of reassurance from their new owners and may take a while to settle down.

From the start of life in its new home the puppy should have a particular place which it can call its own and where it can be made to stay if the need arises. In canine terms the German short-haired pointer is an intelligent breed, which makes it important for owners to establish some authority over the dog from the beginning. Not only do such dogs learn what is wanted of them quickly but they are also fast to take advantage of any weakness in control. Because of its size and strength a young undisciplined German short-haired pointer is a danger both to its owners' wellbeing and to that of anyone else with whom it may come into contact. Clear, consistent, uncomplicated commands should be used from the start, and this applies not only to those dogs destined hopefully for the shooting field but to those which may be kept for the show ring or as pets. It is essential for all German short-haired pointers to receive some obedience training whatever their future may be.

Having emphasised that early discipline is important when taking on a German short-haired pointer, every effort should be made to ensure that the learning process is as enjoyable as possible and a heavy-handed approach is to be avoided. A puppy can learn the simplest, but nevertheless the most important, requirements of a trained dog – to come immediately when called and to sit immediately when told – during the day-to-day activities in its home environment. In fact, with a little ingenuity the owner can make other everyday pursuits part of the early training programme, substituting voice for hand signals or whistle commands and incorporating simple steadiness exercises so that, by the time the dog is able to go out beyond the bounds of the home after its vaccinations are complete, some control will have already been established.

The diversity of work that the dog is expected to carry out means that training the German short-haired pointer is a complex subject and that suggested training programmes can never be strictly followed. Comments and suggestions therefore must be considered in very general terms. Perhaps it is appropriate to mention here that there are very few professional trainers who are prepared to undertake the training of German short-haired pointers. It has been found that, because a confident relationship needs to exist between handler and dog for the team to operate satisfactorily, it is very difficult to get a trained German short-haired pointer totally to transfer its affections to someone other than the person with whom it has gone through the training process. German short-haired pointers are particularly loyal in character and benefit from maintaining the bond established in puppyhood. It also has to be said that the training process never really ends and when dealing with a dog with such energy and enthusiasm reminders will always be necessary. Furthermore, anyone who feels unable to train a German short-haired pointer seldom has the ability to handle it. It follows, therefore, that the best possible person to train the dog is the one who will ultimately be handling it in the field.

The basic requirements of all retrieving breeds of gundog, including German short-haired pointers, are that the dog should walk at heel off the lead, be steady to shot and fall of game, and retrieve tenderly on command. There are a number of books available which adequately deal with these aspects of training. Even more helpful to the German short-haired pointer trainer are the HPR training classes in various parts of the country at which experienced owners can offer advice. Opinions differ as to when each aspect of work should be introduced into the training programme. Everyone has his or her own methods and the experiences to justify them, and so long as the dog ultimately does what is required of it no single method can be said to be right or wrong. It must also be appreciated that dogs are very individual in character and vary considerably even among litter mates in their ability to understand what is required of them at any one time. It is important that the trainer assesses what sort of character he is dealing with and considers his own temperament in relation to this. Above all, before commencing the more serious part of the dog's training, the trainer must know in his own mind what he is aiming for as far as this dual-purpose dog is concerned. Will retrieving be of more importance than pointing? What type of terrain will the dog mostly be expected to work? Will it need to excel in water? The trainer will have to gear his training to these variations. The German short-haired pointer is a dog you can take anywhere but it is unreasonable to expect one used to working hedgerows, ditches and areas of cover to be able to stretch out and work at speed 150 yards either side of its handler on a grouse moor. He will have a good try but will never be as good as one which has worked entirely in that environment.

In spite of their desire for action and involvement German short-haired pointers can easily become bored with repetition as far as retrieving is concerned, and this usually manifests itself in a lazy approach, sloppiness or just plain refusal. New trainers sometimes spend too much time on retrieving, often because they are unsure how to proceed with the hunting part of the schedule and feel that the dog must be doing something. They must remember that retrieving should be given to the dog as a privilege and not a right, and should also bear in mind that too much retrieving concentrates the dog's nose on the ground and this may well adversely affect its hunting ability. Only when the dog desperately wants to retrieve should it be allowed to do so, and then only occasionally!

The German short-haired pointer is above all else a pointer, an air-scenting dog chosen because of that instinctive ability. It will not need to be taught to point, only encouraged to do so and to remain on point for as long as its handler wishes. Dogs vary as to what age they begin to point scent as opposed to pointing on sight and it does not appear to be indicative of ultimate efficiency if they point early or late. Before the need arises for the dog to point scent it must be given the chance to hunt and this is an opportunity for the new owner to leave the retrieving dummies behind and learn to understand or 'read' what the dog is telling him or her. The trainer should simply set the dog off to hunt into the wind on some open ground and do no more than follow and watch its every move. The ability to 'read' one's dog is essential to a good dog–handler combination. The young dog should be allowed to use its nose unhampered by commands from its handler. Later on, when both have more experience, the handler will be able to encourage the dog to work more tidily when it is hunting across the wind, but at no time during its early hunting experiences should the dog be handled harshly. Too much disciplining during this critical learning experience can build inhibitions resulting in the dog perhaps being frightened to get out and hunt. Conversely, a dog with a really tough character might prefer hunting in the next county rather than with a tyrannical handler! It is wise during early training to keep all retrieving exercises quite separate from hunting experience, and indeed it is good practice not to use the same ground for both. In this way the dog can get to know quite clearly what command is for retrieving and what command calls for it to hunt. In addition, even though the dog may have been introduced to gunfire during its retrieving training, it is wise not to combine this with hunting and pointing until confidence has grown and steadiness is assured.

Sooner or later the dog will point and the handler, by now used to 'reading' the dog, will probably be aware by the dog's demeanour that there is something of interest in the vicinity. The handler should now get to the dog's side and gently but firmly encourage it to remain on point for as long as possible. If the bird is well ahead the dog can be encouraged to 'stalk' in towards the bird and hopefully it will point again and 'hold' the bird transfixed by its presence. If possible the bird should not be flushed by the dog in these early experiences, but in any case, whatever happens when the bird gets up, the dog should be made to sit instantly and watch it fly away. The dog should then be put immediately on the lead and taken away so that it will remember that its work for the time being ends on flushing the bird.

In all training, praise for work done well is vitally important.

German short-haired pointers are very sensitive to the moods of their handlers and benefit from shows of appreciation. Equally, an aggressive tone of voice is often all that is needed when reprimanding the dog.

Once it has reached a good standard of ability in hunting, pointing and retrieving, the young dog will be on the threshold of the most important part of its training programme – experience in the field. This transition should be undertaken with extremely unhurried care by the trainer, who should resist the temptation actually to shoot over the dog until he or she has become more experienced at handling the dog in the shooting field. All previous efforts will have been worthless if the trainer allows any slackness to slip into the handling of the dog at this crucial time, and this is inevitable if concentration has to be divided between handling the dog and shooting.

To sum up, the German short-haired pointer has enormous potential as a sporting dog. Its size makes it well able to cope with the largest of quarry and its strength and physique enables it to work tirelessly all day under all conditions. Above all the amiable temperament of the German short-haired pointer makes it the ideal dog for anyone new to HPR breeds. Because of their eagerness to please, German short-haired pointers are to a certain extent able to forgive some of the inadequacies of their trainers, and many end up as useful shooting dogs even when training procedures have been somewhat haphazard. A good German short-haired pointer which knows its job is not simply part of the equipment, it is the most important member of the team. Sportsmen and women having once experienced and enjoyed the co-operation of such a dog want never to be without one.

4

THE
GERMAN
WIRE-HAIRED
POINTER

Marion Jones

ORIGINS AND HISTORY

Let's make one thing clear from the start – the German wire-haired pointer is not simply a furry version of a German short-haired pointer, as so many people seem to imagine. The German wire-haired pointer is a breed in its own right, and an ancient one at that. It was developed by the German hunting masters to be an all-round gundog, capable of dealing with the wide range of game, large and small, from pheasants to wild boar, found on the Continent. The three essentials they concentrated on were coat, stamina and ability.

However, the breed's Teutonic origins are shrouded in mystery and lost in the passage of time. The only certain fact is that it has been developed and controlled by the Verein Deutsch Drahthaar Club, whose experiments with interbreeding and crossbreeding have resulted in an established type. It is this careful control which is the keynote to the future of the breed. The German wire-haired pointer that we see today is the result of centuries of intensive breeding and, provided that care is exerted and the dog remains in the hands of owners who will both work and at least consider showing it, then it can only continue to improve.

Breed standard

General appearance Medium-sized hunting dog with wire hair completely covering skin. Overall should be slightly longer in body, compared to shoulder height.

Characteristics Powerful, strong, versatile hunting dog, excels in both field and water. Loyal, intelligent, sound temperament and alert.

Temperament Gentle, affectionate and even-tempered. Alert, biddable and very loyal.

Head and skull Balanced in proportion to body. Skull sufficiently broad and slightly rounded. Moderate stop, skull and muzzle of equal length with no overhanging lips. Nose liver or black.

Eyes Medium-sized oval, hazel or darker, with eyelids closing properly, not protruding or too deep set.

Ears Medium-sized in relation to head, set high, when brought forward should reach corner of lips.

Mouth Teeth and jaws strong, with perfect regular and complete scissor bite, i.e. upper teeth closely overlapping lower teeth and set square to the jaws, with full dentition.

Neck Strong and of adequate length, skin tightly fitting.

Forequarters Shoulders sloping and very muscular with top of shoulder blades not too close; upper arm bones between shoulder and elbow long. Elbows close to body, pointing neither outwards nor inwards. Forelegs straight and lean, sufficiently muscular and strong but not coarse-boned. Pasterns slightly sloping, almost straight but not quite.

Body Chest must appear deep rather than wide but not out of proportion to the rest of the body; ribs deep and well sprung, never barrel-shaped or flat, back rib reaching well down to tucked up loins. Chest measurement immediately behind elbows smaller than that of about a hand's breadth behind elbows so that upper arm has freedom of movement. Firm back, not arched, with slightly falling back line.

Hindquarters Hips broad and wide, croup falling slightly towards tail. Thighs strong and well muscled. Stifles well bent. Hocks square with body, turning neither in nor out. Pasterns nearly upright. Bone strong but not coarse.

Feet Compact, close-knit, round to oval shaped, well padded, should turn neither in nor out. Toes well arched, heavily nailed.

Gait/movement Smooth, covering plenty of ground with each stride, driving hind action, elbows turning neither in nor out. Definitely not a hackney action.

Tail Starts high and thick growing gradually thinner. Customarily docked to approximately two-fifths of original length. When quiet, tail should be carried down, when moving horizontally, never held high over back or bent. Tail set following continuation of back line.

Coat Outer coat thicker and harsh, no longer than 3.8 cms (1½ in.) long with a dense undercoat (undercoat more prevalent in winter than summer). It should not hide body shape but it should be long enough to give good protection. Coat should lie close to the body. Hair on head and ears thick and short, but not too soft. Bushy eyebrows, full but not overlong beard.

Colour Liver and white, solid liver, black and white. Solid black and tricoloured highly undesirable.

Size Ideal height at shoulder: dogs 60–67 cm (24–26 in.); bitches 56–62 cm (22–24 in.)
Weight: Dogs 25–34 kgs (55–75 lbs); bitches: 20½–29 kgs (45–64 lbs).

Faults Any departure from the foregoing points should be considered a fault and the seriousness with which the fault should be regarded should be in exact proportion to its degree.

Note Male animals should have two apparently normal testicles fully descended into the scrotum. German standard varies slightly. Greater detail is available from the German Wire-haired Pointer Club.

We owe the steadily increasing popularity of the German wire-haired pointer in Britain to the original imports and their progeny, and it is true to say that its unique temperament and ability have swiftly impressed those of the shooting public who have had the good fortune to encounter it in the field.

British servicemen, serving in post-war Germany, quickly came to discover and appreciate the abilities of the breed. One of the first to arrive on these shores was Adda aus dem Potterhoek, which had been bought and trained by Godfrey Gallia in Germany and came back with him when his tour of duty ended. Eventually he decided to secure a mate for Adda but no wire-haired dog could be found and he chose to use a German short-haired pointer, Ch. Blitz of Longsutton. In true Germanic style he concentrated his future breeding plans on the wire coat and other breed characteristics pertaining to the German wire-haired pointer, line breeding and interbreeding to supply his shooting friends with gundogs. This was at a time when the importance of broken pedigree breeding was not considered as important as it is today.

The Germans control such mixed matings very carefully and have rarely, in recent times, found it necessary to go outside the genetic pool of true-bred dogs. No such controls then existed in Britain, the Kennel Club even running two registers – Class 1 for pure breeds and Class 2 for crossbreeds. In 1970 the Kennel Club registered a crossbred dog Chang, by Hector of Raleigh ex Asta.

When the Kennel Club abandoned the two-class system, Class 2 dogs suddenly became true pedigree dogs and this fault is still appearing to this day where the breeder does not fully understand the implications of his or her dog's pedigree. Thus short-hairs, true to type, are being produced from the mating of apparently pure wire-hairs. The breed has enough to worry about in maintaining a high quality of type without having to concern itself with these throwbacks, quite apart from the disappointment experienced by the breeder who had no intention of producing and rearing a litter of short-hairs.

The importance of stock imported over the last few years cannot be sufficiently emphasised. In 1974 Mr Warner imported Vreda vom Romersee, whilst the following year Mrs Birnham imported Hedda van de Reiherbeize and Mr Vaughan expressed a desire to own a German wire-haired pointer. The well-known breeder Mrs Mills de Hoog returned to her native Holland and there secured Rakker van de Mijzijde and Helios for Mr Vaughan and Matilde vant Staringsland to Wittekend for herself. These dogs were all unrelated stock from Germany.

In late 1975 Mr Warner and Major George Wilkinson jointly imported two German wire-haired pointers from the von de Bocholter kennels in Germany. These two, Vicky and Vasal von de Bocholter, were not only brother and sister but also black and white, a totally new colour on the British scene. The genepool, now freshly stocked, produced our modern breeding lines.

The next dog of significance arrived in 1979, a Swedish dog brought in by Mrs Mills de Hoog; this was Mr Allround of Wittekind – or Oscar to his fan club! His character and temperament won the hearts of all those who encountered him. His life was tragically short but he left an influence on many lines. Also in 1979 Major Wilkinson imported the German bitch, Sissi v. Reiler Hals Andersheim. She produced a litter in quarantine of which four survived, Ziggi and Zoe going to Scotland to Diana and Leonard Durman-Walters, Zia to John Birth and the fourth to Ireland, where it was one of the first German wire-haired pointers to be seen.

More recently we have had bloodstock from the USA in the shape of Ch. Desert Mill's Henry Tickencote, owned by Mr and Mrs Howard and Am. Ch. Geronimos Knickers v. SG at Bareve, owned by Mrs and Miss Pinkerton. In 1981 Mrs Mills de Hoog again returned to Holland and this time came back with Macdevil v. de Bemmeraue-Wittekind, the son of the Dutch FT Ch. Quell v.d. Wuppereau. Then the imports to date were completed in 1985 with Arko v. Billetal, owned by Mrs Hilson and Mrs Durman-Walters, and Falk v. Valkenhus, one of the truly classic German blood lines, owned solely by Mrs Durman-Walters.

BREED CHARACTERISTICS AND TEMPERAMENT

An average-sized gundog, the German wire-haired pointer presents a square shape and is capable of crawling through dense undergrowth as well as coping with the unremitting demands of the foreshore. It also has sufficient stamina to deal with the grouse moors. The body should be that of an athlete, with strong, sloping shoulders and a deep chest to provide for plenty of lung and heart room, balanced by a powerful back and quarters.

The coat is a very important aspect of the breed. It varies in length but not in texture or type, and to the touch it must feel harsh and coarse. A close inspection will reveal a dense undercoat which acts as a protection against thorns and brambles and also helps to insulate the animal, particularly when it is working under the bitter conditions which can be a part of wildfowling.

Amongst its most endearing characteristics are the prominent eyebrows, beard and moustache, which, depending on the blood lines, may be more or less pronounced and help to provide the breed's distinctive appearance. The eyes should be a piercing yellow through to dark brown. Light eyes are not encouraged but if the general body pigment is strong then it is only a family trait and not a reduction in genetic strength.

The tail, when docked, should be about one-third of its original length, but as some pups have very long tails it should ideally just cover the genitals. The breed is not docked for fashion but simply for the dog's wellbeing and protection. They are enthusiastic and hard workers, wagging their tails constantly whilst pushing through brambles and thorns. To leave the tail undocked would cause the dog constant pain and suffering as the tip became torn and bloody. The breed is designed for work not the show ring and it is essential that puppies are swiftly and skilfully docked at about three days old. Later amputation is painful and complicated.

The German wire-haired pointer has a very distinctive temperament. It will be aloof and distant with strangers but loyal and loving to its owner. Dogs of this breed make excellent family gundogs when children are present, but have little patience with toddlers. The key aspect of the wire-haired pointer is its sharpness, and it is this facet which must be controlled to get the best from the animal.

It takes both courage and strength to retrieve a wounded Canada goose or bring down an injured deer but the German wire-haired pointer is well capable of both feats. With the working dog the element of natural sharpness must be developed into determination and cunning when tackling game; for the unfortunate creature condemned to life as a non-working pet or the constant round of shows, the inherent sharpness may develop into viciousness. This is due entirely to the frustration of a highly intelligent animal whose chief purpose in life is to act as a hunting weapon. The danger is that, as with so many other breeds, the German wire-haired pointer, if kept solely for showing, will divide into two types – ring and working – and one will be presented with the tall, elegant, bouncy show dog and the more compact, tougher hunting dog.

The breed is willing, bright and desperate to please. German wire-haired pointers are natural hunters, quartering the ground freely, and they are staunch, stylish pointers with excellent noses and the intelligence to work on their own initiative. They should be good retrievers, having soft, sensitive mouths but also strength and ability to hold big game – in fact to bring down a wounded deer or, on the Continent, a wild boar, the most dangerous of all game. In Britain the German wire-haired pointer encounters a wide variety of hunting terrain and work: it may have to act as a very controlled hunter and pointer on low-ground pheasants and partridges, work the grouse moors where its athletic frame and stamina prove essential, or accompany the wildfowler on the foreshore where its thick, thermal coat is of such value. Wirehairs are also used in falconry and deer-tracking (see the later chapter on alternative uses). For a dog to combine these talents requires a special temperament.

I must emphasise, however, that, while for the experienced handler the German wire-haired pointer is a delight to train, the breed is highly strung and not recommended for the novice trainer. A vicious, undisciplined dog is a failure for the breed, the breeder and the unfortunate owner. On the other hand a close relationship between dog and handler will create a rapport which becomes almost telepathic in its intensity. Utter dedication will be given by both parties, and will produce a partnership in the true sense of the word, far more so than with less demanding breeds of gundog.

REARING AND TRAINING

When picking a pup from a litter it is, in my view, best to try and acquire one with all the standard requirements; a shy, nervous puppy will take a great deal of coaxing, whilst one that appears over-bold may call for repressive measures later on. For detailed information turn to the chapter on veterinary aspects of the HPR later in this book.

At six weeks the coat should be relatively smooth with just a few longer hairs, whilst at 14 weeks it should be displaying definite harsh characteristics with some evidence of facial hair. Puppies which appear to be 'fluff balls' will not improve, and smooth, silky short-hairs will remain the same. Appearance does carry proof of the pup's breed history.

The training of the German wire-haired pointer starts as soon as the pup's eyes are open and it starts to wobble about. This breed does not respond if distanced from human companionship so that the best results are obtained when the handler imprints his or her persona on to the young impressionable pup. This should be no later than 8–10 weeks, otherwise the pup may fail to respond. Play, as with all hunting animals, teaches co-ordination, and the pup must be allowed periods of controlled freedom with the handler present to encourage and subtly incorporate a learning pattern into the apparently haphazard games. The puppy will soon begin to grasp the pleasure it can derive from co-operation with its handler. The tone of praise or scolding will swiftly convey your feeling to the dog. Calling it a 'bad dog' in a rough, hard voice will be a harsh punishment.

To control and understand the temperament of the growing youngster calls for tact, psychology and patience on the part of its handler. A simple slap will do little or nothing to gain the animal's respect. This can be acquired only by first obtaining the youngster's trust through constant contact with its trainer and unlimited patience during the repetitive basic training. The pup will very quickly learn to use its brain and show signs of defiance, but with the correct reaction from the handler the pup will realise that it is far better to please than attempt the alternative. Such discipline can vary and may be nothing more harsh than a peremptory shaking with both hands, holding the slack skin of the dog's neck whilst issuing firm commands. The animal must swiftly appreciate that you, the handler, are its pack leader and must at all times be obeyed.

German wire-hairs are very intelligent and remember all too easily when their pride has been hurt. They always prefer to be on the receiving end of praise. Never, at any time, let the dog get the upper hand in an argument, no matter how petty the subject. If you do you are embarking on the first stages of what will prove to be a long and painful road for both of you.

Basic training cannot be rushed and its component parts must become automatic reactions on the dog's part before any other training can begin. Sit, stay and come are the foundation on which all the other elements must grow and it is here that you must endeavour to undertake your subtle balancing act – do not allow the youngster to run wild yet at the same time do not stifle its natural ability and drive. German wire-haired pointers are hunting machines and control should be used only as an extension of basic training.

These dogs thoroughly enjoy learning and the absorption of knowledge so it is all too easy for the trainer to rush lessons in the belief that the dog is more advanced than is actually the case. Rush things and basic training may be partially forgotten, only to be regained by careful retraining. By six months of age the youngster should have absorbed the basic training requirements and be progressing satisfactorily. The moment any element of the basic training goes awry, return to the most basic phases once again until reactions are automatic. However, never, ever expose the youngster to too much training in one day as it will quickly become bored and derive no pleasure from being obedient. Treat the youngster as you would a young child which can concentrate only for short periods without losing concentration.

Exposure to game must also be very carefully controlled and early lessons should take place in an area devoid of rabbits or feathered game. If an older, well-trained dog is available it can prove a help in some lessons, but make sure it does not have any bad manners as these are more readily acquired than good ones. Similarly, training classes can be very useful if the puppy has absorbed its basic training, otherwise they can be a source of humiliation for both of you. On the positive side they provide an opportunity for the youngster to meet other dogs and humans and to acquire a veneer of 'civilised' behaviour.

Hunting is natural to the German wire-haired pointer and there is little that the handler need do. The dog is out there using its nose, and only through gaining a variety of experiences will it be able to assist in filling the game bag. The whistle demands instant obedience and must never be used carelessly or without intending to follow through its meaning. In the early stages of developing the dog's hunting pattern the whistle will be required, in conjunction with a wave of the arm, to turn the dog. Drop the use of the whistle once you are certain the dog is quartering within a set area. The automatic clockwork whistle-turn when hunting is no part of the HPR's natural ability. By all means have the dog turn or stop on the whistle if it has to cross an obstacle such as barbed-wire, but do not teach the dog to hunt on the whistle.

Pointing can only be refined; some dogs lift a front leg, others do not. The essential element is that a point is set and definite. Allow no bouncing or yapping and if this occurs terminate the exercise immediately, returning to it a day or two later. Commands given to the youngster must be unambiguous and must reassure the dog that it is performing that which is required of it. On point the dog can be told, in a firm voice, 'steady'. At this stage do not allow the dog to flush its quarry; this is for the older student because the temptation to chase is always there and can only be controlled with concentrated obedience.

Retrieving needs little teaching as it is an inherent facet of the dog's make-up, but reaching the desired standard of polish calls for patience and tact. The puppy, on being given a dummy retrieve, will bound off happily and return like a ballistic missile, throwing the dummy *en passant* to the exasperated handler. The initial exercises in retrieving will be over a short distance and the dog must sit and stay until the handler is ready; do not allow the dog to take off as the dummy is thrown. Here, because of the short distance involved, voice and hand control are both very important.

If the puppy drops the dummy this is probably due to the fact that it is impatient and also feels dominated by the sheer height of the handler looming above it. Crouch down as the dog returns and show pleasure if the dummy is handed to you. I have even been reduced to wedging the dummy in a soggy mouth, whilst walking backwards, keeping the animal's jaws clenched and gently saying 'hold' at the same time. Gradually, given patience, it will work. Alternatively, as the dog returns I will turn at the last moment and walk away, saying 'heel' and 'hold'. Slowly this will produce the desired hand delivery. It is not a requirement that the dog should sit holding the retrieve in its mouth, but simply deliver it safely to hand and then sit after it has been accepted.

Once the youngster is proficient in basic training, quartering, pointing and retrieving to hand, you can consider entering it in one or two modest working tests. The competition will be friendly and the experience will do the dog a power of good. The emphasis, naturally, must be on control, and do not think of entering unless you are confident in this respect. The quiet, obedient pup will carry out the test without any apparent worry or fuss and may gain a prize-winning score. This is the first reward for all your patience and is ideal preparation for the dog's first season.

Do not rush the German wire-haired pointer's entrance into the real world of shooting; make sure it is sufficiently mature to cope with the temptations of a live shooting day. You will not wish to run the risk of the dog making a fool of you or itself, and perhaps bringing condemnation on the breed from those unfamiliar with it. Initially, half-days are quite enough for the young dog, whilst the presence of a trained older dog will help to reinforce discipline. Do not permit it to retrieve live, warm game on its first few outings as the sheer excitement of the moment may eradicate all the gentleness of mouth which has previously been inculcated. The keeper will thank you for ensuring the dog is kept under close control and at the first sign of over-excitement placed on the lead.

As the season progresses allow the occasional retrieve based on the dog having marked a bird down into ground just beaten out. To receive that first pheasant, neatly handed to you, gives an incredible feeling of satisfaction as you realise that all your hard work is beginning to show results. At first make sure that if you give the command to retrieve you know that either fur or feather, both dead, are there to be picked up. Thus a trust is built up so strong that eventually the dog will search to its last breath if its beloved handler asks it. Leave runners well alone; these are for adults and dogs with experience. A lightly pricked kicking pheasant can ruin a youngster for life.

As far as field trials are concerned, these are for adult, experienced and fully trained dogs. They can be an immense source of fun for both dog and handler but also a source of disgrace and perhaps the ruination of a promising career. Remember that field trials are a test of all the HPR disciplines, including water, and if the German wire-haired pointer, as a youngster, has been encouraged to swim it will perform as though born with webbed feet. Some owners have even claimed that their dogs point while in water!

This, then, is the German wire-haired pointer. I have been proud to own and train two bitches as well as rear ten puppies, all of which have gone on to achieve fulfilment in their particular roles.

Delightful, hard-working dogs, German wire-haired pointers will break the hearts of careless handlers or those who are not prepared to give them full attention. But on the other side of the coin they can prove to be amongst the finest, most loyal and most dedicated all-rounders in the shooting field.

5

THE LARGE MÜNSTERLÄNDER

Geoffrey Hargreaves

ORIGINS AND HISTORY

Ever since its introduction into Great Britain, the large Münsterländer has been surrounded by inaccuracies concerning its origins. The breed's physical appearance is no doubt responsible for the common misnomer of German setter. For, although some large Münsterländers may superficially resemble English setters, it is generally accepted by students and historians of the breed in Germany that there is little evidence that setters of any kind have ever been introduced into the large Münsterländer's background. It is, however, well known that setters, particularly Gordons, were very popular as hunters' dogs in Germany during the last century and doubtless all kinds of experimental matings were tried, as is probably the case with most gundog breeds which we know today. But such hypotheses are academic and it is fairly pointless becoming deeply involved when attention ought to be focused on the breed as it stands at present.

The first breed club for the large Münsterländer was established in Germany in 1919 and, no doubt, this relatively recent date has given rise to the popular misconception that large Münsterländers are a new, recently developed breed. However, even a little research

Breed standard

General appearance   Alert and energetic, with strong muscular body, having good movement with drive.

Characteristics   Multipurpose gundog, ideal for the rough shooter. Excellent nose, staying power, and works equally well on land and in water. A keen worker, easily taught.

Temperament   Loyal, affectionate and trustworthy.

Head and skull   Well proportioned to body, elongated. Skull sufficiently broad, slightly rounded, with no pronounced occiput. Strong jaw muscles, well-formed black nose, wide soft nostrils, slight rise from the nasal bone to the forehead but no pronounced stop. Lips slightly rounded, and well fitting.

Eyes   Intelligent, medium size, dark brown, not deep set or protruding. No haw showing.

Ears   Broad and set high, lying flat and close to the head, with a rounded tip. Hair on the ears should be long, extended beyond the tip.

Mouth   Strong and sound, with well-developed teeth, with a perfect, regular and complete scissor bite, i.e. upper teeth closely overlapping lower teeth and set square to the jaws.

Neck   Strong, muscular, slightly arched, joining the shoulder and chest smoothly.

Forequarters   Chest, wide and good depth of brisket. Shoulders laid well back, forelegs straight, pasterns strong.

Body   Firm strong back, short coupled, slightly wider at the shoulders, sloping smoothly towards the croup and tail. Wide, well-muscled loin. Wide croup. Ribs well sprung, deep and reaching well up to the loins. Taut abdomen, slightly tucked up.

Hindquarters   Hips broad. Well-muscled thighs, well-turned stifles, hocks well let down. Dewclaws should be removed.

Feet   Tight, moderately rounded and well knuckled with dense hair between the toes, well padded. Nails black and strong.

Gait/movement   Free, long-striding, springy gait.

Tail   Well set on, in line with the back. Base thick, tapering evenly towards the tips, well feathered. It should be carried horizontally or curved slightly upwards. Docking of tip of tail optional.

Coat   Hair long and dense, but not curly or coarse. Well feathered on front and hindlegs and on tail, more so in dogs than in bitches. Hair must lie short and smooth on the head.

Colour   Head solid black, white blaze, snip or star allowed. Body white or blue roan with black patches, flecked, ticked, or combination of these.

Size   Height: dogs approx. 61 cm (24 in.); bitches approx. 59 cm (23 in.). Weight: dogs approx. 25–29 kgs (55–65 lbs); bitches approx. 25 kgs (55 lbs).

Faults   Any departure from the foregoing points should be considered a fault and the seriousness with which the fault should be regarded should be in exact proportion to its degree.

Note   Male animals should have two apparently normal testicles fully descended into the scrotum.

quickly reveals that this is by no means the case. By definition, the large Münsterländer is a German long-haired pointer and as such belongs to that great interwoven family of Continental pointing dogs whose history crosses many frontiers on the mainland of Europe and is lost in the mists of time.

During the second half of the last century the move to regulate the various breeds of sporting dog was gathering momentum and many societies were formed throughout Europe and elsewhere for the purpose of improving the quality and standards of available stock. In keeping with this vogue for standardisation, the guardians of the German long-haired pointer, which until that time had always appeared with a variety of coat colours, decided that under the terms of the new rules only dogs with a liver or liver and white coat would be recognised by the German Long-haired Pointer Club. This meant, of course, that the black and white long-hairs had now officially become 'second class citizens'. However, German hunters had long admired the skills of the 'black tigers' as they were sometimes called, a term which clearly indicates the esteem in which they were held, and continued with their support of the 'outcasts'. Gradually this following grew until, with the formation of their own club in 1919, the 'black and whites' attained full breed status.

The name of the breed is derived from the ancient German province of the Münsterländ, wherein lay the flat and at that time marshy region bordering Holland which was the centre of the 'black and white' following. The rather cumbersome name by which we know the breed in English is a direct translation of the German name *grosse Münsterländer*. *Grosse*, meaning large, was included to differentiate from a similar, smaller breed which was developed at about the same time. It is perhaps fortunate for us that large Münsterländers did not originate in an area with a name such as Schleswig-Holstein! As one would expect, the name is popularly abbreviated to 'Münster'. It is interesting, at this point, to note that both of the breed's two cousins, the German long-haired pointer and the *kleine Münsterländer* are, at the present, virtually unknown in Great Britain. No doubt this situation will be changed at some time in the future.

That there is something rather special about the Münster is apparent from the foregoing. The German hunters of old, who were, and whose modern counterparts remain, very exacting in their requirements for a dog, could quite simply have accepted the dictates of the founders of the German Long-haired Pointer Club and concentrated on 'correct' long-hairs, discarding the 'black and whites'. However, experience had shown them that these outcasts had abilities which were worthy of much closer attention and they chose to continue with the dogs which they knew and admired so much. The remarkable fact is that these 'mismarked' long-hairs were capable, purely by their prowess, of impressing themselves upon their supporters to the extent that they won breed recognition in their own right.

Interestingly, the split from its ancestors which brought about the appearance of Münsters has never been total, for German long-haired pointers are periodically used in the breeding programmes of Münsters in their homeland and most British dogs have German long-haired pointers not very far back in their pedigree. It is, therefore, not very surprising that bitches in this country occasionally produce litters which include one or more liver puppies and, although these are not recognised by the large Münsterländer breed standard, they are technically German long-haired pointers. Tricolours also sometimes appear, although these, of course, are not recognised by either breed. The Münster breed standard recognises only black and white coloration, although the two colours are accepted in any proportion and distribution, provided that any white markings on the head are balanced and not too extensive. The standard also provides for the docking of the tail. This is not mandatory, but it is well established that working dogs suffer fewer injuries to the tail if the tip, 1 or 2 cm, is removed as described in the standard.

Officially, the Münster made its first appearance into Great Britain in the early 1970s and, in common with most other HPR breeds, little regard for anything other than their novelty value was given to the early imports. Since that time a total of about 14 dogs and bitches have arrived here from Germany, from which all present stock is descended. It is a tribute to the soundness of German breeding policies that the breed is now starting to develop some semblance of type and consistency in this country. Following a rather erratic start soon after their introduction, the breed was concentrated on by Mrs Pam Perkins whose Foxbrae prefix was so well known in Labradors. Mrs Perkins consolidated the available stock and aided by judicious importations produced a number of dogs which have had considerable influence on the development of the breed.

At the time of writing, registrations with the Kennel Club are running about a hundred annually, which indicates that there are probably about 1,200 Münsters in the country at the moment. Of this total, five dogs have distinguished themselves by winning the highest awards in open competition. The breed's first champion was

Ravenshead Sacha of Raycris, owned by Mr and Mrs Mike and Chris Ogle and Mr Raymond Butler, whose Raycris kennel in Yorkshire consistently produces dogs of quality. The next champion, this time from Lancashire, was Foxbrae Flora of Ghyllbeck, the first and to date the only bitch champion, owned by Mrs Barbara J. Hargreaves of the Ghyllbeck kennel. After this the breed gained its first and only field trial champion in the shape of FT Ch. Clara of Abbotsbourne, owned by Mr John Wagstaff. John has been involved with the breed since the early days and has made a great contribution in demonstrating the prowess of Münsters, particularly in the south of England. Next came Ch. Axel v. Esterfeld of Raycris, again from the Raycris kennel. Axel was imported from Germany as a puppy and has had a strong influence on the breed with the soundness of his progeny. The latest champion is another from the Ghyllbeck kennel, Ch. Ghyllbeck Falco, the first home-bred champion and a son of Ch. Raveshead Sacha of Raycris.

For the benefit of newcomers it would perhaps be useful to explain the differences between the titles referred to and the ways in which they are obtained. Under Kennel Club rules, a dog must be awarded three challenge certificates by three different judges in order to qualify as a champion. These certificates, which are only available at championship dog shows, are awarded by judges approved by the Kennel Club and have printed on them a signed declaration that the judge making the award is of the opinion that the dog in question is worthy of the title of champion. A dog may be awarded any number of challenge certificates during its career but these will not attract any higher accolade. However, breeds which are classified as belonging to the gundog group have one further requirement to meet in order to be recognised as a champion, and that is to provide proof of working ability. Until this is done a gundog is referred to as a show champion (Sh. Ch.).

To become a full champion the dog must win an award at a field trial or gain a show-gundog working certificate, which is a sort of diluted field trial award, in addition to its challenge certificates. This then shows that the dog is capable of performing the function for which its breed was developed, in addition to winning show awards. There are numerous show champion large Münsterländers but these, of course, have no proof of working ability.

The title of field trial champion, however, is attained purely by working ability and is gained by a dog which wins two championship field trials. There is also a further distinction available to gundogs, that of dual champion, a popular name used to describe a dog which has combined the qualifications outlined and won two championship field trials and three or more challenge certificates. This title has yet to be obtained by a large Münsterländer.

BREED CHARACTERISTICS AND TEMPERAMENT

In order to appreciate the qualities which have enabled the Münster to establish the reputation which it today enjoys, it is necessary to have an understanding of the requirements of a German hunter. I use the word 'hunter' advisedly, for that is exactly what the German sportsman is – a hunter in the traditional and popularly understood meaning of the word. For he sets out with dog and gun expecting to encounter any type of game from red deer to partridge and accordingly expects his dog to deal effectively with his quarry, wherever it may be found – whether on marsh, dense woodland or mountain side. These requirements, of course, demand not only versatility from a dog but also, because of the manner in which hunting is conducted in Germany, a high level of initiative, since the hunter expects to meet circumstances where the dog must produce game without assistance from its handler. Moreover, because of the emphasis which the German hunter places on large ground game, dogs are expected to track and retrieve or indicate wounded game which in many instances may have travelled a great distance. This type of work alone relies entirely on the dog's skill and natural ability and obviously dogs which are incapable of performing these tasks are of little use to serious hunters.

In order to ensure that these qualities are maintained in the breed, young stock must attend the annual trials which are held throughout Germany and which are designed to assess every dog in every aspect of hunt, point and retrieve work. These trials are very thorough and require each dog to demonstrate its ability in front of not just one judge but anything up to two dozen, who are split up into groups each of which assesses a different category of work. Every dog is equally and thoroughly examined and must attain a minimum standard of proficiency in each section, including hunting and retrieving, pointing, steadiness, blood scenting and a particularly exacting water test, wherein a dog may be under the judges' scrutiny for up to half an hour.

All of this ensures that the highest of standards are maintained and this is the legacy which we in Britain have inherited. It is the versatility which is so much part of the Münster's character that has enabled the breed to adapt so well to the British shooting scene, even though in this country we do not use HPRs to a quarter of their capabilities.

REARING AND TRAINING

If you decide to acquire a Münster as a shooting companion it is obviously essential that these skills, which have been so carefully nurtured in the breed, are present in the youngster which you intend to train. The best way to try to ensure this is to select a pup from a litter which has been bred from proven working parents; 'proven' being the operative word, for it is amazing what constitutes a good working dog in the eyes of some people. Evidence of one, or preferably both, parents' ability should be readily available in the form of certificates, photographs or even a demonstration. Reliable breeders are only too willing to exhibit the achievements of their stock. Obviously no one can guarantee in what way a young dog will ultimately develop, but if a pup is chosen from a litter bred from parents of unproven ability then the risk of failure is greatly increased.

Naturally, since Münsters are so relatively thin on the ground, the meeting of these requirements may need a good deal of research and travel, and indeed some disappointments, but as is the case with many other commodities, you get what you pay for, or rather you cannot expect the best outcome if you do not buy from the best source. There are few greater disappointments than discovering that a pup is gun-shy or afraid of water, or has some other fault which it may have inherited but which may not have been suspected simply because its parents had never been proved in the field. Many newcomers, and by no means are they confined to Münster owners, make a false start by rushing to acquire a pup from the first litter that they hear about, rather than taking the trouble to learn a little about the breed and what is available before making the choice. They could easily avoid a good deal of worry and heartache by exercising a little common sense and patience.

Patience is the most difficult lesson for a great many people to learn when they become the owners of a Münster puppy. For, rather than gradually learning about the mannerisms and characteristics of their new charges, they so often seem anxious to push puppies along by teaching them ever more complex exercises. Whether the pressure stems from a desire to emulate an impressive older dog which the new owner has admired, or even from the desire to be admired themselves for the dog's prowess, the outcome is invariably the same. I have lost count of the number of times that I have tried to quell the enthusiasm of excited owners who have proudly related stories of their training achievements with their young dogs, performing all manner of control manoeuvres at an age when I would not even contemplate them. However my warnings frequently fall on deaf ears and the next stage of development is that the dog has rebelled and indicated this in the only way of which it is capable, by biting retrieves, disregarding commands or some similar reaction. This usually prompts a blanket condemnation of the breed involved, which is accused of being 'all hard mouthed' or 'totally unruly' when the dog itself is completely blameless.

Unfortunately, it is only too easy to fall into this 'rapid progress' trap, for Münsters, as is the case with other HPRs, possess a high level of intelligence, which enables many of them to pick things up quickly at an early age. This, no doubt, is what encourages the enthusiasm of their owners to push on further until sooner or later the limit is reached. Sadly, by that time the damage is done.

It is absolutely essential that a pup is allowed to enjoy its 'childhood' without any pressure, before entering its 'adolescence' when guidance can be introduced if the dog is capable of accepting it. The important point is familiarisation, for it is during this period that the dog should be encouraged to learn as much as possible about the world around it. It should be gradually introduced to other dogs, traffic, crowds, domestic animals, loud noises, indeed all the thousand and one situations which are commonplace but which could prove unnerving for a young dog to encounter for the first time. Common sense really, but unfortunately a lesson often overlooked by newcomers.

As with all breeds in the HPR group, the Münster has a great deal of knowledge and experience to assimilate if it is to develop to the maximum all the latent skills which it possesses. This, of course, takes time, and experience has shown me that an HPR is about three years old before it can honestly be described as a fully competent dog. Of course there are exceptions as in every other field, but three years is a fair guide as often as not. This does not mean that there is a blank three-year period from when a dog is acquired until it is ready to be used – far from it. It merely represents a steady and gradual process of introducing and exposing the dog to all the situations which it is liable to meet during its working life, until the dog develops into a polished expert able to cope efficiently with any eventuality. It should also be remembered that this must be a reciprocal arrangement whereby the handler learns from his dog through careful observation, thereby strengthening the partnership – I find that Münsters perform far more efficiently working with their handler rather than for him.

The early part of this three-year period should include what I like to refer to as the psychoanalysis time, when the dog's personality must be studied. For, without doubt, dogs have individual personalities in the same way as humans. Some are extroverts, others more retiring; some quick to learn, others less so. It is the observation and appreciation of these characteristics which make it so much easier to produce the desired response from each dog. Whilst this assessment is taking place, the dog should be gently introduced to all the basic obedience lessons, such as coming and sitting to command, walking to heel and all the other little niceties which are so essential to the development of a balanced gundog. The emphasis here is on the word 'gently', for whilst it is essential that the pup must learn obedience, this must be done in such a way that the dog is not inhibited. There is no benefit in having a dog so strictly lead- and heel-trained that it is afraid to leave its handler's side. It must always be remembered that, whilst a young dog is eager to learn and most anxious to please its handler, it is pointless trying to cram its head with lessons which it is unable to absorb. This only causes confusion, which can be permanently damaging to the dog's development. Remember, too, that lessons should always be a source of pleasure to both the handler and the dog. If you find that the dog does not understand or respond in the correct way, or indeed if you get hot and bothered or annoyed, pack it in. It is obvious that you are doing something wrong, either introducing the lesson too early for the dog or approaching it in the wrong way, and persistence can only do harm.

It is also true that a young dog does not learn solely from its handlers, for if the familiarisation period is conducted properly the dog is learning all the time from new experiences, sights, sounds and situations and from other dogs. Bear in mind also that youngsters can learn naughty tricks from other dogs as well as beneficial ones, so be careful to select the company you keep.

The Münster is, as we have seen, a free- and far-ranging hunter, and this ability can easily be stifled by too rigid control. The dog must be allowed to develop this skill by learning to put some distance between itself and its handler; close control can always be introduced when the dog has mastered wide quartering. Of course this requirement does not mean that the dog should be allowed to please itself and run riot. It is up to the handler to select the conditions to permit free running; ground overrun with rabbits or a playing field full of dogs is an obvious recipe for disaster. Once again, common sense must be applied in the selection of suitable situations.

Mention of rabbits raises another very important point, that of chasing game. A young dog must never be allowed to chase game of any sort, for it is a dog's nature to chase quarry and once a pup starts to enjoy this natural instinct it is virtually impossible to correct. Of course this is far more easily said than done, and there has probably never been a gundog worth its salt which has not chased game as a pup. Indeed if a pup is to be brought up correctly and be given the opportunity to observe and enjoy the scent of game, it is virtually impossible to avoid encountering a situation where a chase is inevitable. The secret is to be ever vigilant and hope to anticipate and avert an incident. If a chase does occur, it must be made clear, upon the dog's return, that such behaviour is not favourably regarded and must not be repeated. There is no need to resort to physical punishment for this; stern words and a pointed finger usually suffice, followed by a short spell of restriction on the lead.

Familiarity with dead game and the opportunity to retrieve it is another aspect of training which cannot be introduced early enough. Cold starlings, jackdaws, snipe or any small gamebirds – but not pigeons on account of their loose feathers – are ideal for trying the retrieving abilities of younger dogs and I introduce this kind of exercise when pups are about eight weeks old without any problem. Retrieving and carrying are perfectly natural traits in Münsters and a young dog should always be encouraged and praised for demonstrating it – even though this may entail accepting some particularly nasty and putrid handfuls. A word of caution should be expressed at this point regarding artificial retrieves. Canvas or skin-covered dummies are a useful aid for many aspects of retrieving practice, notably in connection with water work, but many Münsters dislike pretending, resent chasing dummies and quickly become bored with contrived situations. Indeed, the misuse of dummies is the cause of far more problems than is generally appreciated. Once a young dog has demonstrated that it is capable and enjoys retrieving there is little point in flogging away with a dummy and its ever-present risk of an adverse effect; an occasional odd retrieve should be sufficient.

Another item which must be carefully used is the whistle. A whistle is indispensible for dog handling, being far more carrying and distinctive than the raised voice, but it can so easily be misused. A great many handlers employ a complex repertoire of whistles which introduce so many complications that it becomes unclear who is the more confused, the handler or the dog. This effect is apparent on many shoots when, at the end of each drive, a pack of dogs rushes about willy-nilly to the accompaniment of a shrill cacophony of disregarded whistles. In other words, the intended signals have become so confused and repeated as to have no meaning and are therefore largely ignored by the dogs. The message is, keep your instructions, whether by whistle or voice, short, simple and few, but above all each command must represent one instruction and one instruction only, and whatever instruction the signal conveys must be *meant*. Good handlers make little noise.

In conjunction with training classes, many societies organise graduated tests to assess the progress of trainees, and these often encourage handlers to advance to working tests proper. If correctly laid out and organised, working tests can be useful events for giving youngsters experience and for evaluating their progress in relation to other dogs. In fact working tests have developed virtually into a sport in their own right. Many dogs of all breeds have proved themselves adept at the exercises which they incorporate, and form a large following which supports these events throughout the summer months. However, as previously mentioned, many Münsters dislike pretending and rarely shine at working tests. Quite often a dog which appears confused or lethargic when asked to perform in an artificial situation proves to be an expert when doing the real thing – and that is where it counts.

If you and your dog are of a competitive bent you may be inclined to attempt field trials as your expertise as a team increases. Field trials are held throughout the shooting season by most of the HPR breed societies. They are graduated to accommodate differing levels of competence but, since they are designed to follow as closely as possible the conduct of a normal shooting day, it follows that entrants must have attained a reasonable standard of expertise. They are keenly contested and Kennel Club recognition ensures that the awards available do have an intrinsic value. However not everyone, dog or handler, functions at his best under competitive conditions, and some dogs, although excellent workers under normal circumstances, do not show themselves to their best advantage at trials.

When fully experienced and mature a Münster is an unquestioning workaholic, although what we refer to as 'work' is as the breath of life to the dog. In order to maintain its capacity for work it is obvious that it must be kept in good order through proper housing, correct diet and caring attention.

Although very affectionate dogs, Münsters are very robust and do not need, in fact they resent, molly-coddling. If housed outside, the Münster's accommodation *must* be dry and draught-free; heat is not needed. Contrary to popular belief, it is not necessary for a working dog to live outside in order to be kept 'match-fit'. Münsters can take their place indoors as one of the family without detriment, but they do soon over-heat and prefer a cool place to which they can retire.

Feeding is not normally a problem as Münsters have very catholic tastes, but at the same time they are not generally gluttonous. One characteristic of Münsters is their selectivity with food: if offered a titbit, each piece is carefully scent analysed before acceptance and indeed many titbits which are regarded as a delicacy by most dogs are refused by Münsters. An occasional change is beneficial and always appreciated. I prefer to be guided by Mother Nature and feed natural foods when they are available. Raw green tripe is amazingly nutritious and a sheep's head split in two provides numerous advantages – besides simply feeding a dog it also keeps them occupied for hours, exercising the jaws and teeth and keeping the anal glands operative in a way which many 'convenience' foods fail to do.

Minor injuries are unavoidable for dogs which earn their keep, and conscientious owners regularly examine their dogs thoroughly, particularly after a day's shooting. Sheep ticks, thorns, burrs, seeds and so on should be groomed out of the coat, and the feet should be examined for cuts, thorns, split and broken nails and the like, and appropriate treatment applied. Münster's ears are very hairy both inside and out and are a potential trouble source if not examined and treated regularly. There is no need to bathe Münsters habitually to keep their coat in order; in fact bathing can do more harm than good by removing natural oils. Regular swimming and a good old root in the rushes followed by a wash with the garden hose keeps the coat healthy and clean. If a Münster acquires a flea or other parasite this can easily be dealt with by application of one of the numerous available treatments. Diet and health are considered in more detail in the chapter on veterinary care.

If these guidelines, proven over many years, are followed, few problems should arise and many years of pleasure and enjoyment are guaranteed. Versatile, charming, and demanding patience and time from their owners, the taste for large Münsterländers, once acquired, will not easily be dispelled. Once you have been bitten by the 'Münsterländer bug' the disease is virtually incurable.

6

THE HUNGARIAN VIZSLA

Anna Coombe and Sheila Gray

ORIGINS AND HISTORY

The Hungarian vizsla has an ancient and honourable history leading back to the ninth century when the Magyar tribes invaded what is now known as Hungary. With them they brought hunting dogs and it is believed that today's vizsla is descended from a cocktail of these dogs, other native dogs and the Turkish 'yellow dogs'. The Turks invaded Hungary during the sixteenth and seventeenth centuries and it was during this period that the name 'vizsla' was first used.

The word 'vizsla' means 'to seek' in Turkish, though there was also a village in the Danube Valley in the twelfth century that bore the same name. The breed was owned and developed by the sporting aristocracy of Hungary, being primarily used for falconry and it was not until sporting guns were in general use in the seventeenth century that the vizsla was then used extensively for hunting and pointing game. One particular family, the Zays of Zaycegroe, developed and selectively bred the vizsla; today it is believed that most modern vizslas are descended through their breeding.

However, in the nineteenth century a great deal of outcrossing took place, particularly with English and Irish setters, whilst hound blood

Breed standard

General appearance   Medium sized, of distinguished appearance, robust and medium boned.

Characteristics   Lively, intelligent, obedient, sensitive, very affectionate and easily trained. Bred for hunting fur and feather, pointing and retrieving from land and water.

Temperament   Lively, gentle mannered and demonstratively affectionate, fearless and with well-developed protective instinct.

Head and skull   Head lean and noble. Skull moderately wide between ears and median line down forehead and a moderate stop. Skull a little longer than muzzle. Muzzle, although tapering, well squared at the end. Nostrils well developed, broad and wide. Jaws strong and powerful. Lips covering jaws completely and neither loose nor pendulous. Nose brown.

Eyes   Neither deep nor prominent, of medium size, a shade darker in colour than coat. Slightly oval in shape, eyelids fitting tightly. Yellow or black eye undesirable.

Ears   Moderately low set, proportionately long with a thin skin and hanging down close to cheeks. Rounded 'V' shape; not fleshy.

Mouth   Sound and strong white teeth. Jaws strong with perfect, regular and complete scissor bite, i.e. upper teeth closely overlapping the lower teeth and set square to the jaws. Full dentition desirable.

Neck   Strong, smooth and muscular; moderately long, arched and devoid of dewlap.

Forequarters   Shoulders well laid and muscular, elbows close to body and straight, forearm long, pasterns upright.

Body   Back level, short, well-muscled, withers high. Chest moderately broad and deep with prominent breast bone. Distance from withers to lowest part of chest equal to distance from chest to ground. Ribs well sprung and belly with a slight tuck-up beneath loin. Croup well muscled.

Hindquarters   Straight when viewed from rear, thighs well developed with moderate angulation, hocks well let down.

Feet   Rounded with toes short, arched and tight. Cat-like foot is required, hare foot undesirable. Nails short, strong and a shade darker in colour than coat, dewclaws should be removed.

Tail   Moderately thick, rather low set, customary one-third docked. When moving carried horizontally.

Gait/movement   Graceful, elegant with a lively trot and ground covering gallop.

Coat   Short, straight, dense, smooth and shiny, feeling greasy to the touch.

Colour   Russet gold, small white marks on chest and feet, though acceptable, undesirable.

Size Height at withers: dogs 57–64 cm (22½–25 in.); bitches 53–60 cm (21–23½ in.).
Weight: 23–30 kgs (48½–66lbs).

Faults Any departure from the foregoing points should be considered a fault and the seriousness with which the fault should be regarded should be in exact proportion to its degree.

Note Male animals should have two apparently normal testicles fully descended into the scrotum.

was also introduced to increase the hunting abilities of the breed. Despite this, no Weimaraner or German short-haired pointer blood was brought in, as has sometimes been suggested. The first stud book was created by Zoltan Hamvay and Julius Barczy de Barzihaza in 1880.

The demands made upon the vizsla were considerable. It had to be capable of hunting the vast open plains of Hungary for feather and fur and at the same time be capable of dealing with duck and geese, or driving deer towards waiting guns. Not least, the vizsla required the strength and courage to tackle wild boar and wolf at bay. No small demands then, upon the breed.

However, the Second World War and Russian invasion nearly caused the demise of the breed. At the end few of the old, true blood were left and much outcrossing had taken place. Only a dozen or so of the vizsla type could be found and from these sprang the foundation stock of all registered vizslas in Hungary.

The Hungarian vizsla was first registered with the Kennel Club in 1953 by Mr and Mrs Wyndham Harris, who had brought back from Hungary a brother and sister, Ernest and Agnes. Three litters were produced from these two animals, so founding the breed in this country. A Major Petty then became interested in the breed and imported Adalyn von Hunt from America. His prefix, Strawbridge, figured largely in the early days.

Alec MacRae in Scotland was one of the first to use the vizsla as a working dog, training his to field trial standard. In 1956 he imported Tardosi Gyongyi, who features in most of today's pedigrees. She was followed by Sibriktelepi Tigi. It was from Alec that Roger and Virginia Phillips obtained their first vizsla, Creagan Anya. Having previously trained Labradors, they nevertheless produced Anya to awards at German short-haired pointer trials. When mated to Tigi, Anya founded the Kinford vizslas. Each Kinford generation has produced working dogs, and Roger Phillips is a regular judge at field trials.

At about this time, Kinford Vlada joined the Waidman kennels, owned by Major and Mrs Petrie-Hay, already highly successful with working German short-haired pointers. Captivated with Kinford Vlada's character and working ability, Louise Petrie-Hay then found herself totally committed to vizslas, and remains so to this day. Waidman Brok, son of Bella von Wurmbrandpark, who with her brother, Bingo von Wurmbrandpark, were sent to Louise for training, and subsequently offered to her as a gift, probably did more to contribute to the success of vizslas in field trials than any other dog.

Also in Scotland, Evan Young was working his Tintohill vizslas on the grouse moors. He bred Tintohill Astra, who began Mrs Kathleen Auchterlonie's Saline line. Kathleen then imported Szeppataki Czaba from Hungary. Saline vizslas were worked regularly, and figured often in field trial awards. Saline Coire, purchased by Angela Boys from Kathleen, became the foundation of her Galfrid breeding. Fortunately for the breed, having connections in Hungary Angela then imported Matai Sari (of Galfrid) in 1972, who was in whelp to Matai Lurko. This litter, born in quarantine, included Galfrid Gelert, owned by Trevor West, winner of two novice field trials. Matai Sari was followed in the same year by Farad Pusztai of Galfrid, and in 1973 by Matai Vica and Matai Pirok, and in 1977 by Mocsarkereso Vac of Galfrid, thus introducing valuable direct Hungarian working lines.

With the development of the breed, various interested individuals applied to the Kennel Club to form a breed club, and in the late 1960s, the Hungarian Vizsla Club was created, holding its first AGM in 1968. Mrs Petrie-Hay was the first chairman, Mrs Phillips the first secretary and Mr Trist the treasurer. However, after a change of officials in 1970, the members began to feel that genuine support for the club's original aims and aspirations was lacking; consequently, after the 1971 AGM, at which most of the committee were voted off or resigned – it had been established before voting that most of the 'members' present were not vizsla owners – it was suggested a new association be formed. Mrs Auchterlonie then applied to the Scottish Kennel Club to form a Scottish vizsla club, to which the Scottish Kennel Club agreed, but the Kennel Club approval was not granted. Mrs Petrie-Hay, with help from a Kennel Club committee member, then applied directly to the Kennel Club for permission to form a second breed club, explaining the change of motivation and spirit that the new club management was proposing. This approach was successful, the Hungarian Vizsla Society being approved and registered by the Kennel Club in 1972.

The society and the club both, naturally, foster the good of the breed, and each organises annually an open show and a championship show. The society organises field trials from novice to open qualifying stakes, under Kennel Club rules, and both groups put on a working test. Some 20 years after its first recognition by the Kennel Club challenge certificates were first awarded to the breed; now, in 1989, there will be 16 sets of challenge certificates awarded, two sets at the breed club shows and the remainder at general championship shows.

Vizslas have held their own against all-comers. In the 1980s new handlers have taken up the challenge most successfully, Nigel and Sylvia Cox having the honour to train the first field trial champion Viszony of Vallota, whose sire is the great Waidman Brok. Today many more owners work, trial and show their vizslas to the highest level. There are now 11 full champions in the breed, past and present, which compares well with other HPR breeds.

If your personality suits the non-aggressive style of dog, with a short coat, of medium size, able to sit on your lap or drowse happily in front of the fire one minute, but equally happy the next to go out in the cold, damp fogginess of a winter's day on a shoot or a long, frosty walk with or without a gun, then the vizsla may be your choice. On the other hand, consider carefully if you can cope with a dog liable to climb all over you or put its dirty feet on your car in its eagerness to be with you.

REARING AND TRAINING

Before taking on a vizsla you should visit breeders and meet their dogs in their own environment, likely to be the home as the vizsla does not take easily to outside kennelling. Read everything you can lay hands on about the breed. Attend some dog shows where there are classes for vizslas and go to gundog or HPR training classes, albeit without a dog, and see them in action, talk to their owners and compare vizslas with the other HPR breeds.

There is a tendency in the world of dogs which are described as 'working breeds' to make a sharp distinction between working dogs and show dogs, with the underlying unspoken view that the shown dog may be little use in the field and the working dog unlikely to do well in the show ring. There is also, in gundogs, an occasional tendency to equate working only with field trialling. The outcome is sometimes that the shape, personality and style of individual dogs starts to drift away from the lovely creature described above, whilst we struggle to develop one aspect of the dog we consider vital either for the show ring or for working which those on the other side of the fence consider quite undesirable. How sad it is that these distinctions are made, when they are so unnecessary. Work is, after all, a human's word – your vizsla's whole being is concentrated on you, and how it may please you.

This book directs its attention to the HPR breeds as working gundogs. Your vizsla, however, whose nature is to wish to spend all its time with you, will not become an efficient working dog without first becoming a pleasant companion. It takes time, love and endless patience to train the dog from the start so that it behaves the way you wish and remains a loyal, devoted friend. It will be much easier to live and work with your vizsla if it is well handled from the start than to try to correct it later when matters are out of hand.

At all times during the first months, you must be completely consistent, developing your own list of words to be used on each occasion; children and other members of the family who will, of course, play a part in upbringing, must also know their role exactly, and perform it with equal consistency. It is as well to include a release phrase such as 'all right' in your basic list, to let your dog get its food, get up from its sit or down, get in or out of the car, or otherwise stop doing whatever the last command required; the other commands – come, fetch, leave, bed, wait, stay, etc. – are specialised, and covered in detail later.

All dogs respond to an ordered, full life with regular routines, and the vizsla is no exception. Remember, too, that the vizsla is a sensitive, intelligent dog, trying always to do its best for you, so be sure it fully understands what is wanted. Think carefully if the dog is not doing what you think it should be doing – have you made your meaning clear? In general, commands should be positive, single words – 'Oh, do stop pulling!' will get you nowhere – 'No' should be used when there is no positive alternative.

Then, of course, there are the things you should not do, and the natural things a puppy does which should be discouraged – no titbits from the family table, no nibbling in play (the dog nibbling you, that is), no chasing the family cat, preferably no throwing and fetching of balls in the park or garden, and certainly not willy-nilly, no chewing of things being carried about, no pullings things away from it. In fact, say no to anything which you might later wish you had never allowed the dog to do – getting on the sofas and chairs, on the front seats in the car, or on the beds, cocking its leg on your parts of the lawn and garden (if you have 'dog' and 'non-dog' gardens as we do), jumping up at you or visitors, stealing food off the kitchen table or licking the plates. The vizsla quickly learns what is acceptable behaviour, but if you allow it to do these things and later change your mind, resentment and irritation may well be shown – it *will* decide to open the now forbidden door, go upstairs and cock its leg on the edge of your bed or curl up on your best eiderdown, put its feet on all and sundry, or whine at the family dinner table. Paying attention to these facets of education will soon turn the vizsla puppy into a quiet, relaxed animal, ready to undertake the next stage of development.

Give the dog a name which is easy to use, quietly or loudly, and if

Wademan Jaques, a vizsla owned by Mrs L. Petrie-Hey

Ch. Ghyllbeck Falco, a Münster owned by Mr G. Hargreaves

you bred it or can influence the breeder, why not have its Kennel Club name the same as its pet name? Use it from the very beginning; the dog will learn it very quickly and if it is with other dogs, it will know when you are talking to it. Every time the dog is coming towards you, use its name, adding 'come', and make a very big fuss when this happens. As good a way as any at the very beginning is to get down to the dog's level on your haunches, between the dog and its bed, and welcome it into your hands. This prevents the excitable vizsla from jumping up in its enthusiasm to greet you. *Never*, during this time, ask the dog to come when it is heading in the opposite direction; it will surely ignore you and the first fault, needing later correction, starts to creep in. Later on, you are going to need two whistles to work your dog: one gentle pip-pip type used with 'come' or on its own to recall it and also to give it the signal to change direction when it is working away from you, and the other loud, on which you give a short blast as the signal to stop. As the dog gets bigger the double pip-pip can be added to the call to come so that they are connected in its mind.

No doubt as a puppy the vizsla will chew its bed, so perhaps a good start is a sturdy, cardboard box lined with newspapers and topped with the dog's own blanket. The vizsla likes to curl up in a tight bundle, often with its nose tucked under its hip, and the bed should suit this style. Once it has progressed beyond chewing the edges, probably the best thing is one of the newer, oval plastic beds. Put it in a safe corner, out of draughts. You may need two or three in different parts of the house so that the word 'bed' on your list of words can be used wherever you are. If you want to take the dog anywhere, a portable duvet-style bed, becoming very popular now, will retain the same meaning.

Use the accepted training methods to correct uncleanliness in the house, remembering that correction must be gentle, but firm. Our experience with vizslas tells us that, even when quite obviously understanding the need to be clean in the house, they may occasionally quite deliberately be dirty. It seems we are being punished for inadvertently shutting them into a room, or 'neglecting' them in some way. Other vizsla owners have had this same experience, but it has not happened with other breeds we have owned in the same circumstances.

The word 'wait' is usually used for much shorter periods, for example when it is waiting for you to open the car door for it to get in or out, or when you are putting its food down. Teach the dog to sit and wait before its food is given, before you put on or take off its lead, before it gets in the car – in other words, at all moments when you want the dog controlled. You will want the vizsla to stay on its bed for periods during the day and at night, to stay in the car for the occasional period on its own, to stay in another room if you have guests, and sometimes to be tied up to wait outside a shop. Constant repetition of the word and leaving the dog unattended for increasing periods of time will soon have it understanding your meaning. Whilst training the dog to stay in any of these places, try to arrange matters so that you can watch the dog unobserved through the kitchen window, for example, or from inside the house if it is in the car. If the dog fails to wait, go back, put it firmly back in the same place with the same command and try again.

Staying at this stage can be in any position – sitting, lying down or standing up – and the dog can turn around and change position. The criterion is that it should not be wandering about. The stay can become increasingly longer, but must always finish with praise when it has been done correctly; silence is as good a correction as any for failure. However, do not make the mistake with the vizsla of persisting overlong if it is not doing it properly – try again another day, otherwise boredom and resistance will set in. As the dog learns the command, start raising your hand quietly, so that it connects the word with the raised hand. You will need this later to stop the vizsla at a distance.

The lead should be a rope, slip lead, preferably with a 'stop' ring or small strap to keep the neck loop in place, because that is what the dog will wear later. Our vizslas do not wear collars, nor do other working gundog breeds, except when benched for the show ring. A collar can get caught in the undergrowth when your dog is hunting or, worse, snag on a barbed-wire fence causing it to injure itself trying to get free. (Should you want to identify your dog, there is a national tattooing and registration service available at very low cost.)

At first, all you will want is for the dog to walk quietly, without pulling, to your left side. Start by putting a stout piece of string loosely around the dog's neck and let it run about to become accustomed to the feel. Do not leave the dog alone when you start this. Then hold the end and let the dog walk about, progressing to the lead itself. If the dog pulls, although some vizslas never do, a mild jerk on the lead and a firm 'heel' will bring it back to your side. Always remember the praise when something has been done right, and the silence when it has not. Free running at your home is sufficient up to about six months, so do not be tempted to take proper walks on the lead much before this age, even though the dog may be perfectly accustomed to it. However, when your vizsla is old enough to go for walks, take a stick. If you are going to work the dog in whatever capacity, it needs to understand that the stick will do not harm when waved about or thrashed into the bushes; if the dog later goes on an organised shoot with beaters it must ignore the use of the stick in this way.

'Down' is a strong word, requiring it actually to lie down wherever it is, and should be used mainly for longer periods. Use your release word or the next command, together with the raised hand, to let the dog up. Sits and downs should be taught using the accepted dog training methods.

All your initial lessons in sits, downs, waits and stays have probably, till now, been carried out in the quiet of the home, or the car parked in the drive, or in the back garden, where there are few distractions (once the dog has learned to ignore the neighbour's cat). You must then move on to doing the lessons in the local park, the country park or in the farm fields with or without animals (but with the farmer's permission), to get the vizsla steady to all distractions, which may later include rabbits or the running hare. Anyone who has ever attended an obedience class has no doubt heard a class member saying, 'He always does it properly at home!' For the time being, when you start these lessons away from home, the use of the extra long lead (more of this later) will ensure that the dog does not wander off. If you put the dog to stay behind bushes or trees where you cannot see each other and it does take off in the opposite direction, the lead, which you have left lying along the ground, will start to go too. Put your foot on it to stop the dog, then go back, settle it and start again.

As soon as the vizsla has left its mother, let friends and visitors talk to it whenever possible. Then, once inoculations are complete and the dog has become accustomed to being left in the car for short periods at your home, start taking it out, into town, down to the post office, on to a road where it can see the cars go tearing by, to see all the farm animals, and to meet small children if you have none of your own. You may be carrying the dog for it can still be carried at this age. The odd upturned rubbish bin in the dog's area of the garden, or some other unexpected item, such as a brightly coloured lawn mower, barbecue or wheelbarrow, your coat hanging on a bush or the fence, or a waving flag on a stick in your hand, will accustom the vizsla to unexpected sights.

Clapping your hands, dropping a cardboard box, crackling cellophane, knocking saucepan lids together, putting back the lid of the rubbish bin, using the vacuum cleaner or an aerosol can – all these will accustom the vizsla to noise; not forgetting the stick thrashing the bushes as he gets a little older. Start off some distance away from the dog and, as he gets older and more used to the unfamiliar noises, bring them nearer. Gradually introduce the idea that the single sound and the raised hand together mean sit, in readiness for 'dropping to shot' later, when the dog must sit or drop flat at the sound of a gunshot. The same principles will be used when the starting pistol, the dummy launcher (which contains a cap which explodes when it is used) and the sound of gunshot are introduced later.

We have touched on farm animals and the cat, so take the vizsla to basic training classes to meet other dogs and, if you expect to work the dog, try to find a friendly neighbour or farmer who has free-ranging poultry or pet rabbits. The local park will no doubt have ducks, which will come to greet dogs, expecting food. If you live near water, there will probably be moorhens, coots and swans. Any urge to run after them should be curbed, at this stage, with a very firm 'no'. If the dog shows interest, but not to the point of chasing, a gentle 'leave' should be sufficient, with praise if it responds correctly. The age at which the vizsla can start becoming accustomed to other animals will vary with your circumstances – if you have some or all of these animals yourself, it can start as soon as it shows understanding of words. Otherwise, better to wait until the dog is five or six months. By that time it will be able to run faster than you can, so put it on a good, long slip lead folded into your hand; then let the lead out gently so it can go towards them quietly and steadily. At the very first sign of chasing, a quick tug on the lead accompanied by a very firm 'no' should stop it. When it does, lavish praise, then call the dog in and repeat the process. As usual, try to finish the session with the work done correctly, and do not go on too long at one time. If you have access to a pen of rabbits or poultry that is better still, because you can progress through the stages of walking on the lead, then on the long line and finally loose to heel, ultimately leaving the dog sitting there among the animals, expressing not a vestige of interest.

You will also need to start using your stop whistle at a few months old. One short blast has the plain meaning – stop instantly. To start with, add it to the sit or down commands, accompanied by the hand signal. The dog has to be looking at you to read the hand signal and then, if it is going away from you when it hears the whistle, it will turn to see what you want next. A complete disinterest in moving fur or feather which it is not required to retrieve is the total steadiness that you will want. As with all training, it is far better to have the dog absorb the lessons gently and happily now rather than having to use the stop whistle later to make it drop when it has decided to chase an errant hare.

Your vizsla will probably be carrying things about from a very early age. The objects depend to some extent on your lifestyle – from bits of straw or feathers to the post which has just arrived. When the dog first picks it up, it can be encouraged to carry it with 'hold' and it will bring it to your hands if you are at its level and between the dog and its bed. Hopefully it will have picked it up and be holding it very, very gently (a soft mouth). You must take it equally gently, as any tendency to snatch or pull will probably result in the dog hanging on to it – perhaps leading it to hold anything and everything tightly, known as a hard mouth. Lots and lots of praise – you have achieved three things at once here, without actually conducting a formal lesson: picking up, coming when called and retrieving to hand. Praise is just as important when the dog is giving up something you do not want it to have as when it is bringing you something you did want it to have. Although 'give' correctly taught should obviate the need, be prepared to force open the dog's mouth, should the occasion arise.

If everything has gone according to plan, you now have a quiet, socially acceptable vizsla which loves you dearly, as you love it, and which never puts a foot wrong! And you want to take it out to work in the field or enter it in competition. Training classes, preferably for HPRs as not all their training is carried out the same way as that of other gundogs, should have equipment, trainers, locations and livestock, not all of which may be available to you at home. They will also have experience, and there will be other people and their dogs to watch and from which to learn. If, on the other hand, you decide to train at home a second person is often helpful. In addition to your two whistles you will need some canvas-covered dummies, which come in a variety of sizes and weights, from small puppy size and weight to some weighing 6 lbs with different fillings and lengths between 6 and 12 inches. Some are heavy and sag like a dead animal, others are straight. They all float. They can occasionally have a dried rabbit skin or pheasant wing feathers tied round to accustom the dog to the feel of feathers and fur in its mouth.

Retrieving is, of course, one of your vizsla's three basic instincts, but the dog is only actually going to do it when *you* want it to, and not whenever it chooses. When starting the lessons, which can begin in the back garden and later progress to the park or fields, settle the dog down beside you as usual, off lead, tell it to wait and let it see the dummy. Try to make sure the dog watches the dummy's direction and fall as you toss it, and for the first few times go and get it yourself, either walking the dog to heel or leaving it to stay till you come back. Lots and lots of praise if it has done it all right; silence if it has not. It is probably better if the dummy falls into grass long enough to hide it. Remember, it is not the dog's right to retrieve, but a special task required occasionally. Once or twice during each brief session, tell the dog to wait as before, toss the dummy, making sure the dog marks its progress, then tell it to fetch, calling it in with a couple of pips on the whistle as soon as it picks the dummy up. If you are down on your haunches, the dog is more likely to bring it to hand, so tell it to give and gently take it. Do not overdo the retrieving and let the dog actually fetch probably only one throw in three.

You will also want your vizsla to retrieve from water. Hopefully there will be some shallow streams or fishing lakes with shallow edges where you can get it used to the idea of splashing about in the water. As you do not want it to go for the dummy every time, your throwing will sometimes need to be into water where you can wade in and get the dummy, leaving the dog at the edge. The extra lesson to be learned here is that when the dog does carry out a retrieve from water, it does not stop as soon as it gets to the edge, drop the dummy and then give itself a thorough shake. So your earlier lessons of 'hold' come into their own here. Repeat the word, with the dog's name if you like, as it is coming out of the water. Run backwards, encouraging the dog to keep coming, and get down to its level. Hopefully your 'give' and 'sit' will result in the dog giving you the dummy before being released for a good shake. In competition, the dog may have to come several feet or yards out of the water and give you the dummy before shaking, in order to score well.

More advanced retrieving includes the memory retrieve. Tell the dog to wait, throw the dummy, then move off with the dog at heel in a different direction. Walk down the hedgeside or whatever, then turn around and send the dog, using a hand signal, to retrieve the dummy. If it shows signs of not remembering, or appears not to understand what you are asking, go back with it towards the dummy; sooner or later the dog will remember and fetch it. Then there is the split retrieve, taught to remind the dog that there are distractions in life and that the dog is only retrieving because you want it to. In this case the dog goes for the retrieve, of two or three, that you actually want. This reminds the dog that, once on the way to retrieve one bird or thrown dummy, it must not change its mind and go for another bird which may have been shot moments later, or another dummy thrown across its path to distract it.

You will also sometimes want the dog to go back for something that is in the direction it may have just come from. A good way to start this lesson is on a field path. Walk along a little way and, unseen by the dog, drop the dummy, walking on a few more yards. Still facing forward, call the dog in, then turn round, keeping the dog near to heel, and tell it 'go back' with raised arm and a pushing motion of the flat hand. As you are now facing the way you have come, the dog's first thought is that you are going back home, and it will start heading in that direction, possibly coming across the dropped dummy unexpectedly. However, the familiar scent tells the dog there is a retrieve, so it picks the dummy up and you recall it with the whistle and the usual praise. This time, continue the walk in the direction you were first going and drop the dummy again. When you are ready to go home, you can reinforce the go-back lesson by putting the dog with its back to the dummy and telling it to 'go back' for it. Thus the dog learns that 'go back' can be in any direction.

The various facets of the vizsla's learning should be carried out in short happy sessions – a little sit, stay session with the hand signals; a bit of down, with the drop whistle; and a retrieve or two from different positions. For example, leave the dog sitting with the wait command, walk away and then throw the dummy to your side. The dog must, of course, wait without a further command until you tell it to fetch, at which point you introduce your first directional arm signal, clearly raising your arm to show the dog which direction to go from the sit position to the dummy, then the single pip, which the dog will later recognise as the signal to turn, and then two pips to come back in to you and finish the retrieve. This is leading on to hunting, quartering, finding and retrieving game which the dog has not seen drop when shot, and which you want it to go out for, find and bring back. You too may not know exactly where the dead bird is and will have to be able to direct the dog from afar, stopping and turning it from a distance until it scents the bird's location and goes in for the retrieve.

Pointing is the second of the vizsla's basic instincts. The classic pointing stance is exciting to behold – the dog's whole being intent on telling the world that here is something! When it does go on point, at whatever age, move up to it quietly and fold up its front leg if necessary, stroking the dog gently and using quiet words of praise.

Later on, when the vizsla has, essentially, taught itself to point, if there is game around you the dog will also have learned that it 'drops' to the flushed bird, or in other words stays still. However you may not live where there is game and are going to training classes instead. Here it will be taught on caged birds which hopefully will be in a cage from which they can be released to simulate the flush. Once the dog is on point, encourage it forward gently with 'get on', have a blank fired as the bird is released and, if you have to, stop the dog with the stop whistle.

Hunting and quartering, the dog's first hunting, is likely to be along the hedgerows and into the copses when it is out walking with you. The dog will, by its very nature, be investigating every lovely smelling bush and hole and getting its nose up in the air too, to scent the passing wind. Use an encouraging word – 'find it' or similar – being ready to stop the dog with the whistle should game be flushed. Although the hunting comes naturally, however, actually quartering an area of ground in a pattern needs to be taught. It is best to start in a small area, perhaps a patch of land hedged on either side, preferably without the distraction of live game. Stand in the middle and let the dog go off towards the hedge, which it is likely to do naturally. When it reaches the hedge blow the stop whistle. When the dog turns to look at you, give one pip (the turn signal) and an arm direction to get it going in the other direction. When the dog has crossed in front of you, and is about 10 or 15 yards to the other side and front, repeat the stop whistle, turn whistle and hand signal to send it back diagonally in front of you to the other side again. On the training sessions we hope there is no game, but in competition or on a day's rough shooting, the dog will need to quarter the ground, zig-zagging across it. You are then directing the dog to use the wind to carry scent across itself which it will then quickly find and go on point.

One day will come the time when the dog does something forbidden and you are absolutely sure it has not misunderstood your instructions – although the reason for the lapse will not always be apparent. The vizsla does not need a beating. If your silence has not been enough to convince the dog that you do not like its behaviour at all, or your tone of voice does not make it clear, try grasping the scruff of its neck on both sides immediately behind the ears and giving it a good shaking. But be absolutely sure that the dog knows what it has done wrong, and make the punishment immediate.

We hope after reading this chapter that you will select a vizsla, and perhaps work it, but whatever happens teach it to be a pleasant animal to have around. The vizsla will be a most loving and gentle friend to you if you are to it.

7

THE WEIMARANER

Edward Hardman

ORIGINS AND HISTORY

There are as many theories about the origins of this elegant grey sporting dog as there are patent cures for the common cold. Like the patent cures many of the theories have common ingredients but to a great extent thereafter you pays your money and you takes your choice. Without delving too far we find the Grand Duke Karl August of Sax-Weimar-Eisenbach in his state capital Weimar hunting game with these streamlined grey dogs in the late eighteenth century. How they came to be there produces claims from the French for the Chien gris de St Louis, a royal hound during the thirteenth, fourteenth and fifteenth centuries, and a further claim via the St Hubertus hound bred by the monks of the St Hubertus monastery in the Ardennes. Claims that the English pointer contributed cannot be discounted since the royal court of Hanover was populated with English nobility and their dogs, including pointers and setters, for the majority of the eighteenth and nineteenth centuries. Throw in the Spanish pointer claim, that of the Great Dane, the Hanover bloodhound and the mastiff and you have the perfect EEC dog. The Hungarian claim that the vizsla is a forebear of the Weimaraner can be balanced by as many claims that the Weimaraner is a forebear of the vizsla.

Breed standard

General appearance   Medium sized, grey with light eyes. Presents a picture of power, stamina and balance.

Characteristics   Hunting ability of paramount concern.

Temperament   Fearless, friendly, protective, obedient and alert.

Head and skull   Moderately long, aristocratic; moderate stop, slight median line extending back over forehead. Rather prominent occipital bone. Measurement from tip of nose to stop equal to measurement from stop to occipital prominence. Flews moderately deep, enclosing powerful jaw. Foreface straight, and delicate at the nostrils. Skin tightly drawn. Nose grey.

Eyes   Medium sized. Shades of amber or blue-grey. Placed far enough apart to indicate good disposition, not too protruding or deeply set. Expression keen, kind and intelligent.

Ears   Long, lobular, slightly folded, set high. When drawn alongside jaw, should end approximately 1 inch from point of nose.

Mouth   Jaws strong with a perfect, regular and complete scissor bite, i.e. upper teeth closely overlapping lower teeth and set square to the jaws. Lips and gums of pinkish, flesh colour. Complete dentition highly desirable.

Neck   Clean cut and moderately long.

Forequarters   Forelegs straight and strong. Measurement from elbow to ground equal to distance from elbow to top of withers.

Body   Length of body from highest point of withers to root of tail should equal the measurement from the highest point of withers to ground. Topline level, with slightly sloping croup. Chest well developed, deep. Shoulders well laid. Ribs well sprung, ribcage extending well back. Abdomen firmly held, moderately tucked up flank. Brisket should drop to elbow.

Hindquarters   Moderately angulated, with well-turned stifle. Hocks well let down, turned neither in nor out. Musculation well developed.

Feet   Firm, compact. Toes well arched, pads close, thick. Nails short, grey or amber in colour. Dewclaws customarily removed.

Tail   Customarily docked so that remaining tail covers scrotum in dogs and vulva in bitches. Thickness of tail in proportion to body, and should be carried in a manner expressing confidence and sound temperament. In long-haired tip of tail may be removed.

Gait/movement   Effortless ground covering, indicating smooth co-ordination. Seen from rear, hindfeet parallel to front feet. Seen from side, topline remains strong and level.

Coat   Short, smooth and sleek. In long-haired variety, coat 1–2 in. long on body, somewhat longer on neck, chest and belly. Tail and back of limbs feathered.

Colour   Preferably silver-grey, shades of mouse- or roe-grey permissible; blending to lighter shade on head and ears. Dark eel stripe frequently occurs along back. Whole coat gives an appearance of metallic sheen. Small white mark permissible on chest. White spots resulting from injuries not penalised.

Size Height at withers: dogs 61–69 cm (24–27 in.); bitches 56–64 cm (22–25 in.).

Faults Any departure from the foregoing points should be considered a fault and the seriousness with which the fault should be regarded should be in exact proportion to its degree.

Note Male animals should have two apparently normal testicles fully descended into the scrotum.

The uses to which the Weimaraner was put in its early days in Continental Europe confirm the need for a good basis of hound blood. The ability to track live and wounded wild boar and deer and to use air scent when in proximity to the quarry were essential houndlike characteristics which bridged the gap between hunting in a pack and providing sport for the gun-carrying sportsman. Undoubtedly, as the application of these talents to gamebirds became more necessary with the changing pattern of the sport, the temptation to introduce pure 'bird dog' blood would have been too great to resist.

The Weimaraner crossed the Channel to this country for the first time in 1952 when two British officers leaving BAOR, Major Bob Petty and Major Eric Richardson, succumbed to the German claim that this dog was a combined bird dog, retriever, coon dog, rabbit dog, watchdog, personal guard and house pet. Since that year, when a total of 15 Weimaraners were imported, the popularity of the breed has increased to the point where the number of registrations with the Kennel Club is now more than a thousand a year. Alas it is not the breed's ability as a gundog that accounts for this rapid increase but its appeal to the showing fraternity. The very striking and unique colour, the aristocratic and elegant bearing and the natural instinct for showing off make the breed a popular show dog and unfortunately a status symbol for some whose town environment is totally unsuited to an active gundog. However, around the country there are Weimaraners working hard and happily as gundogs and rewarding their owners by their skills and persistence.

BREED CHARACTERISTICS AND TEMPERAMENT

Of the HPR breeds, the Weimaraner is probably the least stylish hunter and with its tendency to carry its head lower than the other breeds it suffers in competitive dog work by comparison with the others. In Germany it is recognised that the breed is different from the much wider-ranging breeds (German short- and wire-haired pointer, Brittany and vizsla) and it is grouped separately for field trials with the Münsterländers. The Weimaraner's tracking ability and persistence are greatly prized, along with its ability to deal with wounded deer and wild boar, and despatch foxes and wild cats. The Germans also require the breed to demonstrate a controlled ability as guard dogs. These innate instincts and abilities have to be harnessed and adapted to use as a gundog in this country and it will be clear to most people that these attributes add up to a unique breed that requires unique methods of training in some areas of its work.

Probably due to its hound background the Weimaraner is a gregarious soul which hates loneliness and, living up to its American name of the 'grey ghost', will be happiest following its owner around, not necessarily getting involved in the same activity but just being 'with'. This hatred of loneliness will often show itself in boredom and destructiveness.

In spite of some of their less endearing country habits, including a penchant for cowpats, Weimaraners have very sensitive stomachs and require considerable care with diet, a subject to which we will return. On the other hand, innate greed is also a breed trait and makes Weimaraners some of the most inveterate thieves on earth. However recently or substantially fed, few grey beasts are able to resist any form of gastronomic temptation and the word 'enough' is unknown in their vocabulary. In a volume about working gundogs it probably goes without saying that the combination of a voracious appetite and a lack of exercise will produce a fat, sluggish and unhappy dog.

The Weimaraner also has a reputation for aggressiveness and indeed there are some unpleasant, aggressive and plain evil dogs, often the result of careless breeding of one doubtful temperament to another. However, despite what you may read to the contrary, it is possible to own a Weimaraner which will pile happily into a beaters' trailer with many assorted dogs and people and which will share its home peaceably with other breeds. It would be prudent, nevertheless, for the first-time Weimaraner owner not to attempt to keep a male Weimaraner with a male of another breed.

REARING AND TRAINING

For the potential Weimaraner owner probably the best way of finding a suitable puppy is to see a good Weimaraner at work and to approach its owner to discover where it came from and how it was bred. Alternatively an approach to the secretary of the Weimaraner Club of Great Britain will elicit details of litters and breeders of good working stock.

To some extent it is true that there are strains of the breed in this country where the working instincts are more likely to be present and developed to a higher degree, but the breed is fortunate in being relatively young in this country and in not having separated into the working type and the showing type. One need not run a mile from breeding which has a show champion or two in it because the standard for the breed against which show dogs are judged is the conformation required to enable a hunting dog to keep going all day and to do the job it was created for. There is no need in the Weimaraner pedigree for the inbuilt suspicion of show champions such as has developed among spaniel and retriever owners, whose breeds have split into the show type and working type to the point where they are virtually separate breeds. It is worth noting that the only two Weimaraners which up to now have ever qualified for the championship field trial also have show challenge certificates to their credit.

More importantly, the shooter should take as much care over the selection of a puppy from stock of the right temperament and a pleasant disposition as searching the country for the offspring of two Weimaraners which work every day of the shooting season. The rewards and applause of completing the finest piece of dog work are going to be substantially diluted if this paragon of working dogdom flies at every other dog which tries to get into the back of the same Land Rover.

The best age to assess Weimaraner puppies and to try to picture what the adult dog will look like is between five and six weeks. Thereafter there is a period until the puppy is about six months old during which the puppy will go through the cuddly, foldy stage into the period of gauche and awkward adolescence. Its feet will be too big, it will have too many legs, its skin will not fit and it will be about the most uncoordinated creature on earth. It is definitely a Weimaraner trait that until six months the young dog is often a disorganised heap and very rarely a miniature Weimaraner.

Do not take a puppy from a nervous, shy litter which runs for cover at the mere sound of a human voice. However, do not be put off by finding one puppy fast asleep in a corner whilst all the rest of the litter are rioting. It is quite likely that that sleeping puppy had gone on rioting longer than the rest during the last mob-up and is now recovering whilst the others have started the next tumult. At all times be guided by the breeder, who should be spending plenty of time each day with the pups and is in a far better position to assess their individual characteristics. Any breeder worth his or her salt will want to try to match the right pup to the right owner. The breed is not riddled with, but neither is it free from, hereditary defects such as hip dysplasia, and searching questions should be asked to be sure that the breeder has taken all hereditary defects into consideration in his breeding programme.

To sum up, you cannot buy a good working Weimaraner off the shelf. Be prepared to do a great deal of homework, choose a breeder you feel you can trust and be prepared to be patient.

Your troubles with the small dog with the big feet and ill-fitting skin do not start when you get home. They start on the way home in the car. Young Weimars are inclined to suffer from car sickness and if the pup is consigned to the back of the car on its own this problem is even more likely. The breeder will usually not feed the pup before its first journey, so try to arrive at the arranged time. Take a towel or two and some newspaper, and if possible take a willing passenger in whose lap the puppy can sit. A sudden and violent event may well happen after only a few miles, and thereafter a good deal of dribbling, but do not be put off or think that this is an insurmountable problem. Take the pup in the car with you wherever you go and before you realise it you will have a dog that actually enjoys being there. In bad cases your vet will prescribe a mild sedative and with persistence, particularly with a few long journeys, the pup can be completely cured of car sickness.

Before leaving the breeder you should have discussed and received a diet sheet and perhaps some of the food the pup has been reared on to see you over any gap between collecting the pup and being able to buy the same food. At all costs avoid a change of food on top of a change of owner and environment. Weimaraners, as we have seen, have sensitive stomachs. An over-rich diet can have a disastrous effect on their digestive systems and make the task of keeping them reasonably well covered a difficult one. The many brands of complete food either in pellet or meal form seem to suit them best and although the food has a very plain and boring appearance their innate greed seems to prevent palate fatigue. For a finicky eater some raw green tripe can be added. Veterinary advice seems to be increasingly in favour of such complete diets for puppies and there are several brands with special puppy complete feeds which include all the nutrients needed by a growing dog in the right balance. The practice of feeding large quantities of food and vitamin supplements to rear quickly maturing puppies ready for the show ring at six months is increasingly coming under suspicion of leading to bone diseases such as osteochronditis and Maur's syndrome which afflict young dogs. The puppy's diet is considered in more detail in Chapter 11.

Ensure that if you have to leave the dog on its own there is nothing vital that it can reach that is easily destroyed. This applies also to bowls and beds. A plastic water bowl, apart from being easily tossed about, will soon have puncture holes in it and a basketwork bed which looked so cosy in the pet shop will soon look like a cross between a

Wild West stockade and a crown of lamb. The best bed for the potentially destructive Weimaraner is the plastic 'indestructible' one and even then a determined or bored beast can give one of these an attractively scalloped edge. The other advantages of this type of bed are the lack of draughts and its slight clearance above the floor. Once the chewing stage is passed a bean bag makes a very acceptable bed.

The Weimaraner's short coat provides it with little warmth and so it is less suited to kennelling through the winter unless some heating, and possibly a more hairy companion, can be provided. But if you do wish your Weimaraner to live outside then start as you mean to go on. If you have allowed it to get used to living indoors, it will no doubt protest vociferously at being relegated to an outside kennel.

Beyond the fact that it has a delicate stomach, loves human company and chews plastic water bowls, the Weimaraner's early upbringing has no requirements which are not common to most gundogs. It is becoming increasingly recognised that if a puppy is to grow up into a well-balanced adult plenty of human contact is essential from a very early age. Washing machines, banging cupboard doors, vacuum cleaners should all be part of the learning process.

There must be no doubt in the young Weimaraner's mind that you, its owner, are also its boss/pack leader. This does not mean that every time it moves a muscle you must clobber it, but if it shows any signs of challenging your authority in a physical way a short, sharp reminder is called for. There is nothing unusual in a small woman being totally dominant over a large male Weimaraner simply by sympathetic and consistent training, and it is equally possible to see a large man totally at odds with a Weimaraner through over-harsh and thoughtless upbringing.

The young Weimaraner at five to six months is old and strong enough to be introduced to the delights of hunting ground with game scent on it. Let the dog run free as you walk into wind and do not worry about it chasing game. Steadiness can be introduced at a later stage when the young dog is beginning to put together the component parts of its hunting, pointing and retrieving trade. Above all, the inclination of the young dog to get interested in gamefinding and using its initiative in this direction must not be stifled by over-emphasis on control and blind obedience. With a bit of patience these can be introduced later. This may sound like a recipe for disaster but I have known many dogs who have benefited from some freedom in their first year and have had their rough edges smoothed off later. I have never met a Weimaraner which, once trained to a high level of obedience and control, has subsequently been introduced success-fully to the delights of hunting.

I am not proposing for a moment that the young dog should receive no training at all. The need to have this large grey beast behaving reasonably well is obvious – no home would survive the ravages of a wild, destructive, unsociable dog. The local canine society obedience classes will give the new owner an insight into how to create a domestic animal out of a potential hoodlum. But when the dog will sit and stay in view of the handler, walk to heel on and off the lead and come when called, that is the time to leave the classes well alone because the next stage of obedience will begin the process of destroying initiative in the hunting dog and leaving all the thinking to the handler. The introduction to retrieving can be left fairly late in the training process since the Weimaraner is more often than not 'carry-mad'. The lure of early success in working tests with a polished young retriever may lead the dog into being too controlled too young.

For all that its skin looks like that of a seal the Weimaraner is not a natural water dog. Gradual and sympathetic steps are needed to increase the young dog's confidence, starting with some shallow water of no more than Wellington boot height. Get the dog to join in some jolly games at no more than standing depth and this will improve the dog's enjoyment of water and guarantee the handler a pair of wet feet. Then find a river with a gradual entry and a helper who will hold the dog on one bank until the owner has bridged, forded or swum across to appear on the opposite bank without the artful dog having seen the method of crossing. If the dog has any feelings in the owner's favour it will walk into the shallow water towards its owner and begin swimming. Care must be taken not to face the dog with either too wide or too fast-flowing a river or too steep an entry. As many different bits of river as possible must be found since a dog, whilst appearing to be confident in a familiar spot, may funk a new piece of water. Endless harm can be done by trying to force a young dog into water, particularly in mid-winter, when the danger of ice on a pond and the sheer discomfort will be obvious to the dog even if the handler is trying to ignore them.

Another area where Weimaraners have a less than perfect reputation is that of hard-mouthed retrieving. There is nothing in the breed which guarantees either a hard or a soft mouth and those who have seen an excited and pleased dog take its owner's hand in its mouth and lead the owner by the hand will find it difficult to believe that a Weimaraner could be hard mouthed. Those who have been offered a flat pheasant will keep their hands to themselves. The owner's hand is an object of care and affection to the dog and the aim should be to persuade the dog to treat everything it retrieves with the same care. The throwing of sticks and twigs for a dog to retrieve will certainly help to undermine this intention. There are, indeed, those who advocate the practice of putting part of the hand into the dog's mouth when first introducing the dog to cold game.

All these apparent shortcomings in the breed might give the

embryo field trialler the feeling that trying to trial a Weimaraner would be like shovelling water uphill – hard work at all times and never likely to be completely successful. It is true that until the 1988 field trial season no Weimaraner had ever won the top level of field trial, an open qualifying stake, and yet within the month of November 1988 the same dog won two open stakes to become the first field trial champion in 36 years of the breed in this country. It could be argued that one field trial champion in every 36 years is unlikely to persuade those who enjoy competition to choose a Weimaraner, but the new emphasis in the revised Kennel Club field trial rules requires judges to recognise the differing styles of the different breeds and to judge the dogs by comparison with the ideal for each breed rather than by comparison of one breed style with another.

The Weimaraner is a strong, loyal and affectionate companion both in the home and in the shooting field. It needs a lot of food, time and exercise but will repay the investment of these by being the ideal rough shooter's dog. Regardless of the scarcity of grey field trial champions there are lots of happy owners with sensible Weimaraners up and down the country, working their dogs in the beating line, picking up behind the guns or doing what every Weimaraner enjoys most, walking up game.

Anyone who is out at work all day leaving the dog in an empty house, anyone who does not like walking or anyone who requires from a dog the response of an occasionally animated door mat or hearth rug should not have a Weimaraner. If the requirement is for a working gundog which is reasonably easy to train to an acceptable level as a versatile, all-purpose dog, but which is unlikely to be a field trial champion, the Weimaraner is a sensible choice.

8

FIELD TRIALS

Brian Finan

In the early 1950s, the owners of HPRs in Great Britain (at that time essentially German short-haired pointers) wishing to enter them in field trials had to be content with running in pointer/setter trials. They acquitted themselves very well in these, but of course such trials tested only a part of hunt, point and retrieve work. The German Short-haired Pointer Club therefore organised the first field trial for dogs which hunt, point and retrieve, and this took place in 1954 at Brandsby Hall in Yorkshire. In 1963 the Kennel Club granted championship status to field trials for dogs which hunt, point and retrieve.

Since these early beginnings hunt, point and retrieve field trialling has gone from strength to strength, with a great number of trials being run by various organisations. Indeed, the problem for most handlers nowadays is to decide just how many of these trials one can afford to enter.

THE TRIALS

All gundog field trials conducted in the British Isles are governed by Kennel Club regulations, and are divided into four sub-groups:

(1) retrievers and Irish water spaniels;
(2) sporting spaniels other than Irish water spaniels;
(3) pointers and setters;
(4) breeds which hunt, point and retrieve.

The Kennel Club definition of a field trial is 'a meeting for the purpose of holding competitions to assess the work of gundogs in the field, with dogs working on live unhandled game, where game may be shot'. This is a very concise explanation of the *raison d'être* for field trails. However, the reasons which would be advanced by the participants to explain their involvement in field trials are many and varied. Field trials provide the showcase through which can be seen just what can be attained by a well-trained dog of a particular breed. Good judging of trials both sets and should help to raise standards, not only for triallers and trial dogs but for handlers and dogs in the everyday shooting field. For competitors trials are a yardstick, measuring both through the judges' and the competitors' own eyes the amount of success or failure of his or her training methods. Trials provide education for spectators, allowing them to learn by example, to improve their own handling by emulating the good work, and to avoid the consequences of the less than perfect performance. For breeders, scenting ability, drive and determination, game sense, biddability, consistency and willingness to face cover, fences, water or other obstacles are all facets of gundog work which cannot be properly assessed in a kennel yard; a good field trial will provide a thorough test of all these attributes. These are but a few of the reasons which make the organisation of, or running in, field trials worthwhile. However, one aspect upon which I have not yet touched, but which to my mind is as important a reason as any other, is that field trials are *fun*.

The foregoing remarks would, of course, apply in any of the four sub-groups for which the Kennel Club sanctions field trials. Although some of the following could similarly apply to sub-groups 1, 2 and 3, we will now look at sub-group 4 and essentially devote the remainder of this chapter to field trials for dogs which hunt, point and retrieve. All the dogs described in this book can, and indeed do, run in trials for dogs which hunt, point and retrieve. At the time of writing all breed clubs, except Italian spinones, run trials.

The people responsible for organising field trials for these breed clubs are the hardworking field trial secretaries, whose tasks include arranging field trial grounds and liaising with field trial hosts, inviting judges, organising food and accommodation for judges, guns and officials, compiling and distributing field trial schedules and entry forms, receiving the completed entry forms and fees, arranging the ballot for running order in the trial, seeing to each trial on the day, and handling field trial matters in general which crop up throughout the year.

Schedules and entry forms for field trials are sent out to paid-up members of societies before the beginning of each shooting season. If one is not a member of a particular society it is usually possible to acquire a copy of that society's schedule by writing to or telephoning the field trial secretary. Sometimes, but not always, schedules are sent to handlers who are not members, but who ran in the previous year's trials of that society. The way to make sure of receiving your schedules, of course, is to join, in good time, any society in whose trials you intend to enter.

These memberships, of course, carry with them all the usual voting rights and will ensure receipt of information regarding forthcoming events, newsletters and any other publications. Added bonuses which are usually gained by full membership are reduced entry fees and the entitlement to hold any cups or trophies which one may be fortunate enough to win. Some societies have rules which restrict entry or give preference to members in certain trials.

The schedule

The schedule lists: date and venue of the trial (with directions to the meeting point); judges; type of stake (i.e. novice, all-aged or open); number of runners; date on which entries close; time, date and venue of the draw (the draw can be witnessed by intending runners to ensure fairness, though this is rarely an option taken up); entry fee; any trophies which are available. Enclosed within the schedule will be a brief explanation of the rules and regulations governing all stakes. Also enclosed will be several entry forms. Newcomers to field trials will find that field trial secretaries are only too happy to advise on the completion of entry forms.

The rules and regulations

An attempt to analyse and explain all these rules and regulations in detail is well beyond the scope of one chapter in this book, and therefore I shall attempt only to shed some light on matters which are of interest to newcomers to the sport. The full rules and regulations concerning field trials are contained in the *Kennel Club Year Book*, part III, and intending field triallers would be well advised to obtain a copy, available from the Kennel Club for a modest fee.

The sections of the *Kennel Club Year Book* which apply to field trials are basically split into two parts: the Kennel Club Field Trials Regulations and the Guide to Conduct of Field Trials. Whilst there is an obvious need to be familiar with the Regulations, I would strongly advise intending triallers to familiarise themselves fully with the Guide. Here will be found the formula for successful participation in field trials.

Stakes

The following are definitions of certain stakes (Kennel Club Field Trials Rules and Regulations):

> *(1) Open.* A stake in which dogs have the opportunity of gaining a qualification (whole or part) for the title of Field Trial Champion or for entry in the Championships or Champion Stake for its breed and in which entry is open to all dogs of a specified breed or breeds. It may be limited to a prescribed number of runners, in which case these shall be decided by a draw where preference must be given to previous performance.
>
> *(2) All-aged.* A stake which is open to all dogs of a specified breed or breeds without restriction as to their age, but which may be restricted by any other conditions which may be determined by the Society.
>
> *(3) Novice.* A stake which is confined to dogs which have not gained the following awards:
> First or Second or Third in Open Stakes, or
> First or two Seconds in other Stakes.
>
> *(4) Puppy.* A stake which is confined to dogs whelped not earlier than 1st January in the year preceding the date of the Field Trials. (For such stakes run in January, a dog which was a puppy in the previous year shall be deemed to be still a puppy.)
>
> Other Stakes may, with Kennel Club approval, be promoted by Societies, but all Stakes must be clearly defined in the schedule.

Those are the four definitions of Kennel Club stakes. We will examine them in reverse order, starting with puppy and working up to open.

Puppy
For our purposes, and in line with common practice, puppy stakes can be disregarded as I know of no society which currently runs a puppy stake for dogs which hunt, point and retrieve.

Novice
A novice stake is a competition for dogs which are inexperienced in field trials, but it is certainly *not* the place to be for a dog which lacks experience in the field.

Dogs running in novice stakes can be, and often are, subjected to all the same situations which need to be faced in the higher stakes. At the start of each day's trialling we are reminded of the guidance given to judges that 'a trial should be run as nearly as possible to an ordinary day's rough shooting'. This means that, as we will be working with ground game and birds in their natural environment and not in contrived situations, little or nothing can be done to ease the burden placed on the dog and handler partnership.

However, judges will try not to run dogs downwind (although this may sometimes be necessary) and will look more sympathetically at any misdemeanours or failures which may occur in a novice stake. The difference between novice stakes and other stakes comes at the water retrieve, which is a contrived situation and therefore can be made easier for novice dogs.

All-aged

An all-aged stake is generally understood to be a stepping stone between novice and open stakes where extra field trialling experience can be gained and where judging will generally be more strict than in novice trials.

Open

This is a stake which should be entered only by the very experienced team of dog and handler. Judging in these stakes will be very strict and will allow little room for error by either member of the partnership.

Although there is no rule insisting that dogs must have been in novice or all-aged stakes before entry can be made in an open stake, it is accepted by most triallers that the lower rungs on the ladder to the top are the novice and all-aged stakes. In any case, any attempt to reach the peak without first scaling the lower slopes is likely to be thwarted by the preferential draw system which some societies organising open stakes now apply. The maximum number of runners allowed is 12 dogs for a one-day stake and 18 dogs for a two-day stake.

Subject to the following, a Society may give preference to its own members.

Preference in the draw for Open Stakes for all Sub Groups except Retrievers

Preference in the draw for Open Stakes must be given in the following order:

(a) Members' dogs which have gained a First, Second or Third award in an Open Stake or a First or two Second awards in other stakes.
(b) Non-members' dogs which have gained a First, Second or Third

award in an Open Stake or a First or two Second awards in other Stakes.

(c) Members' dogs, which have gained other awards.

(d) Non-members' dogs which have gained other awards.

(e) Other dogs.

The foregoing awards must have been gained in a Stake qualifying for entry in the Kennel Club Stud Book during the season then current or in the two seasons preceding it.

The Hunt, Point and Retrieve Championship

The Hunt, Point and Retrieve Championship is a two-day trial which is run annually. The winning dog in this trial becomes a field trial champion unless it already holds that distinction. Entry is by invitation only and invitation is currently extended to field trial champions (including Irish field trial champions) and dogs which have won a first or second place in open qualifying trials in the previous season or in the current season up to the closing date for entries. The number of runners in this trial is reviewed annually by the Kennel Club.

Basic requirements

Dogs shall be required to quarter ground in search of game, to point game, to be steady to flush, shot and fall, and to retrieve tenderly on command from land or water.

Again, a concise description of what is required, but for the inexperienced trialler this needs to be examined more closely.

Quartering, which in our case means *hunting*, is a very important aspect of an HPR's work. Without efficient quartering gamefinding will be less productive. Without a 'find' there will be no point, without a point there will be no controlled flush, without a flush there will be no shot and fall giving the opportunity to show the dog's steadiness and its ability as a retriever. All these facets of the dog's work are important in field trials, and must be demonstrated to give the judge the opportunity to mark them. Hence the real need for hunting to be of the very best.

Judges will often advise you at the start of your run to 'make sure that you cover the guns'. Do not fall into the trap of assuming that they are asking you to run the dog from gun 1 to gun 4, passing guns 2 and 3 on the way. Due regard must be paid to the wind and the judges are in fact asking the dog to search the air in front of the guns with its nose. This is done most efficiently with the dog running at 90° to the wind and not necessarily at 90° to the direction of advance.

Likely looking game-holding areas must be thoroughly checked.

However, do remember that good dogs not only indicate the presence of game, they will also show a handler that ground is bare; if this is the case do not carry on beating out this piece of ground until dog, judges and guns eventually show their disinterest. Trust your dog once an area has been covered thoroughly without result, and get on smartly to fresh ground.

Do not hesitate to ask the judges to hold up the line of guns at any time you feel that the dog has not yet covered your ground. It is your run, do not waste it. You will be required to inform the judges when you consider your dog to be pointing or indicating the presence of game; this is done with a raised hand. Great caution must be exercised at this stage to avoid a premature flush, before guns are in position. Although the judges will strive to ensure that guns are correctly placed, it will be to the advantage of the handler to ascertain that this has been done. The command to flush must only be given having been ordered by the judge. Steadiness must be of the very highest order in a field trial dog, and once having been instilled must always be maintained. Steadiness to flush does not necessarily precede steadiness to shot and to fall, therefore handlers must at all times be attentive to the dog and be prepared to take corrective action should there be any movement towards unsteadiness. When the bird is safely on the ground, and until the order is given to retrieve, this vigilance must be maintained. Many a dog has eliminated itself by prematurely retrieving, without command, minutes after the bird has hit the ground and when the handler has turned to speak to the judge.

Quiet, confident handling at this stage is the most likely way to achieve a tender retrieve. Only commands which will be of help to the dog should be given, based on sound knowledge of the shot game's whereabouts. Noisy handling will serve only to confuse the dog, not impress the judges, and may well move on game in the next part of your beat.

Competing

> Dogs shall be run singly in order of draw under two judges judging as a pair. A dog must have been tried twice in the line, excluding the water retrieve, before it may receive an award.

Mostly self-explanatory as it stands, but of necessity rather a brief description. Reams of paper could be filled about the running of a trial, but to shed a little more light on the way the competition is conducted the following may be useful.

Dogs are run singly in order of the draw for the first round, after this judges are able to see dogs in any order they may require to enable them to reach their decisions. These decisions are arrived at by the two judges deciding together, but marking separately, each category of work on which a particular dog has been tested during each run.

That a dog must be tried twice in the line does not necessarily mean that it will be tried *only* twice in the line; indeed the guide to judges states that 'They should see as much work as possible from every dog, particularly those which impress most favourably and assess this work carefully in every aspect.' Depending on the circumstances of each individual trial, dogs can be called several times up into the line.

As has already been mentioned, the water retrieve in a novice stake is different from the water retrieves in other stakes. Dead pigeons are usually used at the water. For novice dogs, the pigeon is thrown into the water and a shot fired, while in other stakes the pigeon is required to be retrieved from across water, unseen and without benefit of shot.

Faults

Eliminating faults:

> Hard mouth – whining or barking – flushing up wind – out of control – running in or chasing – failure to hunt or point – missing game birds on the beat – refusal to retrieve or swim.

Major faults:

> Not making ground good – missing game on the beat – unsteadiness – sticking on point – persistent false pointing – not acknowledging game going away – failing to find dead or wounded game – catching unwounded game – disturbing ground – noisy handling – changing birds or other game whilst retrieving.

Some of these points we have already covered and some need no further explanation. I will pick out one or two to clarify. Flushing up wind (better known as 'bumping') is where a bird is flushed without the dog pointing or indicating and where the judge considers the wind was to the advantage of the dog and should have been pointed or indicated. In missing gamebirds on the beat (eliminating fault) and missing game on the beat (major fault) there is an obvious distinction between flying game and ground game. However, both cases are very difficult decisions for a judge. In the first instance this presupposes that all birds remain absolutely still except when disturbed by dog or man. To my mind there is always the possibility of a bird walking in behind the dog and subsequently being flushed by the spectators, although of course this is not always the reason for missed birds and as in all other matters it must be left to the experience of the judges to make a sound decision. In the case of missed ground game it is a well-known fact that hares in their form give off so little scent as to be virtually undetectable, and in my experience it would be a very hard judge indeed who would set much store by a missed hare.

AWARDS AND PRIZES

Needing no explanation, here is a reproduction of the Kennel Club's system of awards.

(a) An Award is any placing in a Stake decided by the Judges which may be First, Second, Third or Fourth. The following may also be awarded at the discretion of the Judges:
  (1) At a Championship or Champion Stake meeting, Diplomas of Merit.
  (2) In any other Stake, Certificates of Merit.

(b) A Prize is a reward for merit in competition.

(c) All Prize Money must be paid within one month of the date of the Field Trial, and paid subject to return in the event of a subsequent disqualification.

(d) The amount of Prize Money offered by a Society may be varied to relate to the number of entries received and may be reduced if the full number of entries is not received.

(e) Equal awards for any prizes offered at a Field Trial are prohibited.

(f) The Judges are empowered and instructed to withhold any Prize or Award if, in their opinion, the dogs competing do not show sufficient merit.

At some trials there will also be a 'guns' award' which may take the form of a bottle, a brace of birds, cash or whatever, which the guns kindly give usually to the dog that they have enjoyed watching and shooting over the most, although on occasions the award has been known to go to the happiest-looking dog, the most amusing dog or the most unfortunate dog.

SHOW GUNDOG WORKING CERTIFICATE

It must be mentioned that for dogs which have won one or more challenge certificates in the show ring a system is available whereby the dog can become a full champion and thus remove the 'Sh.' from

'Sh. Ch.' The rules governing this operation are contained in the *Kennel Club Year Book*, and are almost as long as all the other field trials put together. The essential points on which the judges must satisfy themselves before awarding this certificate are that the dog hunts, points, retrieves tenderly and enters water and swims. Steadiness is not essential.

In practice very few people avail themselves of this facility, perhaps due to the fact that most dogs which are capable of fulfilling these basic requirements have been trained on until ready to enter the trial proper, where any place or COM will also remove the 'Sh.'

'GIVING IT A GO'

Well, now you have reached the stage where your dog has completed its basic training, is handleable, steady and under control in all situations, and you have probably run in some working tests. The dog has now had experience in the shooting field proper, has hunted for, found and pointed game, flushed, watched it being shot and retrieved tenderly. All this will have been done in a variety of situations and at different locations. Now you feel that you would like to enter a trial. My advice to you is don't! Unless, that is, you have already attended at least one, and preferably several, trials.

By watching and learning about trials before entering, a lot of heartache can be saved. This was very clearly illustrated when someone who is now a well-known handler completely threw away his chances in the first trial that he entered by not being *au fait* with the system. Having overcome this setback, the partnership's results in the next five trials that they entered were five wins in a row – one novice, two opens (which made the dog into a field trial champion) and two hunt, point and retrieve championships.

So before you consider entering, go to trials as a spectator, particularly novice trials. Look at the standard that you have to beat. Be honest with yourself – can you beat it? Listen to, and ask questions of, experienced handlers, especially those with an enviable track record. Watch and listen to the judges, try to understand what they are looking for in their winners, get the feel of a trial day before you put yourself up into the front line.

Having done all this, do not forget to sieve any information that you may have gathered so that only the good advice is acted upon.

There is no reason at all why this watching and learning process cannot be going on alongside your basic dog training, or for that matter before you get your dog. Indeed it would help in schooling the young dog, in that the handler would have a more positive idea of what is required of the fully skilled field trial dog.

SPORTSMANSHIP

One of the great pleasures of trialling is, in my opinion, the very fine atmosphere of sportsmanship which prevails – each and every competitor not only hoping for a good performance on the part of his own dog, but also looking forward to seeing good work from all the other competitors in the trial. With this in mind, very genuine good wishes are passed on as dogs and handlers go forward into the line. On returning after a successful run, congratulations will await the partnership, whilst heartfelt commiserations will go to teams where circumstances have been less favourable.

It is to my mind a great pity that so many other so-called sports do not share the camaraderie which is associated with field trialling and, indeed, with all country sports.

Having said all this, it does not for one minute mean that friendly rivalry is excluded from our sport. It would be a poor field trial that passed without some good-natured banter playing a part in the day's proceedings.

Another aspect of the pleasant nature of trials, especially in these days of things being taken for granted, is at the end of the day to see individual competitors, whether winners or losers, going round shaking hands, thanking the host, guns, judges and stewards for the day, although this has of course already been done officially in the end-of-trial speeches. It goes without saying that this is also the time for personal congratulations to the award winners.

SPECTATING

Spectators are generally welcome at field trials, subject of course to obeying some very basic and commonsense rules.

Do arrive in plenty of time, not just reaching the nearest village for the start time, but in time to find the actual meeting place. This may be one particular field, which I can assure you will look exactly like all the other fields in the area when you are in a hurry. You will also need to allow time to dress in suitable clothing, which in the shooting season is usually something warm and waterproof. Muted colours, i.e. greens and browns, are best. The dayglow oranges, reds and blues may be useful for those who find their pleasure in falling from boats or mountain sides, but dog handlers looking for partridges will not be best pleased to see these colours amongst the spectators. Stout and waterproof footwear is essential, and a good strong stick is as good as another leg.

Safety is of paramount importance in field trials, as it is in all other forms of shooting. To this end spectators will be asked to stay close at all times to an official carrying a red flag. This allows the guns to shoot into what they will know are safe directions. Should anyone for any reason need to leave the trial ground before the end of the trial, it is only common sense that one should first of all ascertain, from the steward of the beat, the gamekeeper or the red flag person, not only which is a safe route but also one that will not interfere with the rest of the day's trialling. Late arrivals will need to make very careful reconnaissance indeed to ensure that neither the trial nor themselves are put in jeopardy. Handlers should take note that, as well as complying with these requirements, the permission of the judges or the chief steward must be obtained before leaving the trial ground. Spectators are asked not to bring dogs on to the trial ground.

In conclusion, may I say to newcomers to the HPR breeds that we are in an almost unique position in the gundog world of having dogs which fit the breed standards and are still capable of performing the work for which they have been bred. This dual standard must be maintained. To this end a better understanding of the dog's work must help in future breeding programmes. So whether or not you intend to trial, do come along and have a look. I can guarantee you a friendly welcome and an interesting day. For those of you who decide to take the plunge I wish you good hunting, and ask you to keep up the standards and always to remember that it is only a game!

9

SHOWING AND WORKING

Gay Gottlieb

As far as Great Britain is concerned the HPR breeds include the German short-haired pointer, the German wire-haired pointer, the Weimaraner, the Hungarian vizsla, the large Münsterländer and the Brittany spaniel. These breeds were specifically and painstakingly developed and bred in their countries of origin to perform a particular task.

The sporting nobility of Europe, with their vast estates and extensive variety of game, required an all-purpose dog, one which could cope with differing terrain and game. Such dogs would be required to quarter the ground wide or close according to prevailing conditions, find game, staunchly point and on order flush, mark the fall and retrieve on command, from land or water. The dogs would work not only on game and wildfowl but also boar and deer. Such breeds or types of dog, the HPRs, were thus developed with enormous skill and care.

It is important to note that each of these six breeds has its own characteristics and that each is unique in appearance, conformation, colour, type, style and method of working. Each has its own standard set in its country of origin, and as it has been imported into this country it has been registered and classified by the Kennel Club of Great Britain. There is no reason at all why the structure of these

HPRs should be altered and it is essential to understand that one and the same dog can fulfil the necessary requirements for bench and field.

All breeders must take heed of the standard, without prejudice, since it is the blueprint based on the original prototype; those who know and understand how to read a pedigree will also be all too aware of the hazards of breeding the wrong type. For example, the correct coat is essential in a gundog. No silky, thin, soft coat will stand up to punishing cover, a cold winter's day with the north wind biting or rain driving in sheets across the plough.

The standards state that the German short-haired pointer's coat must be short, flat and coarse, whilst the Hungarian vizsla's coat is short, dense, coarse and greasy. The large Münsterländer's coat, although long, must be dense, whilst that of the German wire-hair, a distinctive coat, must be long and strong enough to protect the body. Its facial whiskers – a very particular feature – are intended to protect its eyes and mouth. The Brittany must have a dense coat. It thus becomes clear that the texture of the coat is vital when the dogs are being worked.

It is interesting to note, on speaking to owners of these six breeds, who work their dogs through the shooting season, that they have few worries about injuries or poor condition and, in fact, if they show them, have little preparation to undertake for the show ring. Obviously a poor doer will present problems, whether it is worked or shown or both. It is essential that these dogs are given the highest quality food and care if they are to look and perform at full potential.

Working gundogs cannot be kept under wraps and no keeper or gun would for one moment brook pathetic excuses – 'Sorry my dog has a show tomorrow so I don't want him to go into thick cover where he might get scratched.' From the breeder and owner we are asking for excellence of a high order, good stockmanship, total dedication to the dog and a knowledge of how it should look and work.

HPRs and their owners are nothing if not versatile. One will tell you of wildfowling one day and on the following winning best of breed at Crufts. Another of working his dogs on difficult northern terrain, with sharp rocks and 5ft-high stone walls topped with barbed-wire, and then winning best of breed at a championship show two days later. Another owner will recall beating with his HPR one day and taking a 3rd ticket the next. But the following must surely qualify for the *Guinness Book of Records* for sheer versatility: picking-up on Thursday, winning a challenge certificate on Friday, winning a field trial on Saturday and a working test on Sunday – all this with the same dog!

Where work is concerned the smooth-coated HPRs seem to have no more trouble coping with the hazards of injury when working than

Eldridge Bettina, a Weimaraner owned by Mrs G. Tranquada

Adam from Hapsburg, a GWP owned by Miss C. Green

do the longer coated breeds. For all handlers, though, the major nightmare in the countryside is barbed-wire. A strong fence of sheep wire topped by two or three strands of tight barbed-wire between dog and a strong runner creates a heart-in-mouth situation.

Apart from potential tears on barbed-wire, the most common problems to be dealt with are thorns, briar and bramble scratches, ticks, nettle stings and sore feet. And even if these minor hazards are avoided, at the end of a hard day the dog will look tucked up and exhausted. The dog must be looked over carefully and rubbed down, given a hot, nourishing meal and a warm bed. With a good night's sleep, it will be ready for more work the next day. Few HPR owners would dream of bathing the dog, either after working or before a show. It is essential that the coat remains greasy and a shampoo will immediately destroy this protection.

The Brittanies and the large Münsterländers, because of the amount of white in their coats, do present more of a problem, and both they and the German wire-hairs tend to leave some of their hair behind on brambles so that by the end of the season the true working dog will have less coat than the show dog. However, most good judges will take this into account.

Most owners of working dogs have their own specific remedies for the hazards of a shooting day. Surgical spirit, Dettol or salt water may be used for cuts, scratches and sore feet, while vinegar provides relief for nettle stings. One vizsla owner carries an Acromide puffer which she claims is 'good for wounds', whilst she also uses a homoeopathic medication called Hypercal and gives her dogs large doses of vitamin C if they shown signs of flagging during the season. Many of us keep a few Mars Bars in our pockets; these provide a high source of carbohydrates which dogs can easily absorb. In conditions of extreme exertion a deficiency of glycogen can result in pain and fatigue. (See Chapter 11.)

Let us suppose that you are a complete novice at showing and working but that you would like to have a go at both aspects; you have taken good advice from specialists in your breed and, most vital of all, you adore your dog, you suit it and it suits you. 'This is the real trick of success' as an old friend often tells me. Your puppy is going to reach the top in the ring and gain every accolade in the field. Keep this dream in front of you and, although you may not achieve it, at least you are on your way.

The great joy of the HPR is that the dog loves to please you and share your life and this is a great start. Elsewhere in this book you will discover aspects of training particular breeds, but the following will give you a solid foundation for showing the dog.

First of all, do not be deterred by those who warn you that if you work your dog its conformation will be ruined. If the conformation is correct in the first place by the time the animal is ready to do a full day's work it will be physically mature. Of course there are always those who push their youngsters too far and too fast, but no puppy should be over-exercised at any time. In my breed – vizslas – I have seen better fronts in the field than in the show ring and I am sure this is due to natural selection. A badly constructed front and poor flat feet are no help on hard, tough going, and therefore such dogs are less likely to be used for work. Nor would they be bred from to work.

The HPRs are gregarious, great lovers of comfort and highly sociable. Many people are amused to find that the 'show/working gundog' adapts its lifestyle to whatever its owner desires. One day it may sleep in its kennel or stable or rough it in the back of a car; the next it may be found sleeping in the kitchen or the bedroom. There is no need to wrap the dog in cotton wool, and though it loves to lie by the fire it is just as happy prancing in snow. Thus the ease with which it adapts to any change of circumstance greatly assists it when both showing and working.

THE IDEAL SHOW CAREER

You own your first HPR and you are really pleased with it. You have no idea whether it is good enough to show except that the breeder said it was a good one. If the breeder said it will make a good show dog and you bought it at 7 to 8 weeks old, that breeder must have knowledge that no other has – at that age it is impossible to be positive since an HPR goes through many stages. At 7 or 8 weeks old you think you have a world beater, but at 10 weeks it can look as if it has every fault in the book.

It is a sensible idea to visit a local show or two, just to observe and glean information. Find out what is expected of you and your dog, and talk to the show goers. There is a wealth of facts you will need to know, so here are a few to start with.

A puppy cannot be shown before it is six months old. For its first entry choose a small show, an exemption or local open show. You will find it easier and more relaxing, the competition not nearly as formidable as at a championship show. Novices frequently enter their puppy in every class available. This is not sensible. It is tempting but a young puppy can tire quickly and become bored, so only enter it in one or two classes if you want it to enjoy the day. Aim to arrive early, giving yourself plenty of time to familiarise yourself and your puppy with the atmosphere and the place. For your HPR's debut, you will need to equip yourself with:

- your admittance card and schedule;

- safety pin or metal tag for pinning on chest to hold class number;
- money handy for buying a catalogue at show (this is vital because it tells your bench number, ring number and all essential information);
- bag for carrying the following:
  show lead
  rubber glove
  velvet duster
  benching collar and lead
  blanket (for dog)
  water and water bowl
  food for dog (and something for you too!)
  clothing for snowstorms, pelting rain or a tropical heatwave!

So you have been to your first show, and you enjoyed it. Whether you won a prize or not you have acquired a taste for this side of the dog game. You now try to gain as much experience as you can, entering your puppy in small shows with a championship show in mind in a couple of months' time. Remember that some championship show entry applications must be received two months before the show date.

Depending on the classification for your particular breed, there may be a puppy and a junior class. If not you will have to enter it in the first one or two classes that are offered. If you have found that your puppy is a natural, loves every minute of showing and is an extrovert, you could enter the puppy stakes, but if it is likely to weary and become bored do not risk it.

When you have reached championship show stage your puppy will have had some good wins in the smaller shows that you have been to, so although nervous you will probably have gained confidence and a certain aplomb. You know that your puppy is not shy, it may stand and will trot if in the right mood! Even so, neither of you will have been prepared for the noise and tension, the magnitude of the place and the thousands of dogs and people. You will have the opportunity to compare different types and lines that you have heard and read about. You will meet the breeders and enthusiasts and some of your puppy's relatives too, perhaps.

We will suppose that your puppy wins both its classes. Now you can feel that you may have something good! You will then have to compete with all the dogs who have won their classes. That means you are up against the winner of the open dog class who, as likely as not, is a show champion or a champion, so you would not expect to beat that dog at this stage. But as you come out of the ring, you should be feeling very pleased. Stay and watch the other dogs being judged. Find out who does win the open bitch class. Then the best bitch, having won her challenge certificate, competes with the best dog who won his challenge certificate. Find out which of the two will get best of breed and go on to compete in the gundog group against all the best of breed gundogs.

At this stage the tension mounts round the ringside – everyone playing at judging and trying to guess which one will be put up. The two challenge certificate winners are standing perfectly in the middle of the ring, the strain telling as you see the hands of the handlers shaking, their faces serious, not a muscle moving. The judge asks them to move their dogs again – he is finding it a difficult decision. They both stand again, the judge goes over to the table, collects the best of breed card and rosette and gives it to the dog's handler. Everyone relaxes, both the dogs and their owners, and the crowd claps. The judge has a brief chat with the owner, then the winners do a lap of honour and come out of the ring amid congratulations. When that happens to you for the first time, you will never forget it.

Suppose that it does happen to you a year or so later and it is you holding the precious prize, your dog's first championship certificate. You have gained your junior warrant and qualified for Crufts. You have worked your way up from puppy classes to junior, maiden, novice, to post graduate and limit and finally, if your HPR gains its third challenge certificate, its title will be show champion. It can only enter the open dog class after this. Generally the competition in this group is really hot because it will be competing against the other champions and show champions in the breed.

By this time you have done a lot of winning – and losing too, so you know what it feels like to go cardless. You have managed to smile even so and to be gracious to those who beat you, even if you felt it was not justified. But, more important, you have asked questions, been modest and sensible enough to take good advice and recognised virtues and faults in your dog. Your handling has improved and you feel that it is a good partnership between you and your maturing dog. Perhaps it has been through a stage of listlessness and boredom when you had to lay it off showing for a time, having no training and no show lead. Good walks and a bit of fun tend to cure this problem and the dog should come back as if it had been on holiday and start to show again with a liveliness and energy for the job.

Some of your friends and competitors will have experienced similar difficulties with their bitches. Invariably they 'go off the boil' when they have been in season and during what would be the gestation period of nine weeks if they were in whelp; their minds are on nests rather than show rings!

You need to gain two more challenge certificates before you can call your dog a show champion. You will find it difficult not to take everything too seriously; your showing days are not the naive win or

lose days that you felt in the beginning. Now they are tinged with not
a little cynicism and wariness, as well as a deeper understanding of
people and dogs. To recognise that you are ambitious and need to win
is important, if it goes hand in hand with the ambition to gain more
knowledge of your breed and a wish to see your dog find a place with
the best in the ring and in the field.

When you have gained your third challenge certificate you have to
go into the big ring. If you go into that ring expecting it to be a piece
of cake, you will not have learnt a thing on your way up! If you know
that it is very, very unlikely that you will even be pulled out in the last
six or eight then you have learnt a lot. If you understand what your
chances are you have come a long way from the day when you first
showed your puppy. You have assessed your dog as a judge should,
not as a novice.

WHAT THE JUDGE WANTS TO SEE

The judge assesses the conformation of the dog to the specification of
the standard. He can best achieve his final decision by examining the
dog standing in a show ring posture and when the dog is gaited, so
that he can see how the structure of the dog functions in action.
Therefore to allow the judge to see your dog at its best advantage you
need to understand how to place and move it correctly. So firstly we
will discuss the different ways of handling and how to set the dog up.

Setting the dog up

With your dog standing on your left-hand side, hold its muzzle with
your left hand, place its right foot, then change over, placing its left
foot parallel to the other; check that the feet are in line with the tip of
the elbow and the top point of the shoulders; this will immediately
demonstrate the angulation of the shoulder and forequarters. Holding the dog's head, either by the muzzle or with its lead up behind its
ears, run your left hand over its back in order to place its back legs so
that they too are parallel to one another; bend down and reach for one
leg and then the other. They should be so positioned so that when
viewed from behind they are straight and when viewed from the side
the dog presents a balanced picture, covering the ground adequately,
demonstrating the correct angulation, the hocks being perpendicular
to the floor. Check the balance again by stretching the head and neck
slightly; the dog will adjust its weight so that it is distributed correctly.
Finally position yourself so that you have control of the dog's head
and forequarters with your right hand and hold its tail (horizontal)
with your left hand. Thus your dog should feel relaxed and com-

fortable because its whole body is being correctly supported. Smooth its back every now and then, and talk to it, so that it knows that it is pleasing you.

Practise opening your dog's mouth. This is necessary because the judge should always look at the teeth. Once the dog becomes accustomed to your handling, it should not mind a judge going over it.

How to gait your dog

Your dog has to learn to trot by your side. This is the pace that demonstrates the dog's structure functioning at its most effective. The judge will instruct the handler to trot his dog in a triangle and in a straight line so that he can assess the dog's movement from different angles, its stride, topline and ground covering ability. When practising, place the lead up the neck whilst keeping the head at the same level throughout; the lead should be neither too tight nor too slack, thus the dog remains 'collected'. The pace should be a 'moderate but lively trot' and the handler can best do this by synchronising his pace and the dog's in order to move as one. Keep it 'going forward' at all times when it is gaiting, and do not allow it to pull away from you, otherwise it will not be balanced and it will start to crab, creating problems in movement. Always keep the dog between you and the judge. Be attentive to the judge's wish if he requires a triangle, use as much of the ring as possible and trot your dog into the corners. When going straight, make sure it is not a diagonal! Never allow your dog to 'run into the judge'. Stop a few feet away from him, keeping your dog standing as alert as you can on a loose lead – this is when all the faults show up because you do not have a chance to pose the animal. If your dog can do all this with its tail wagging it will indicate its happy temperament and will be a pleasure to watch.

How to spoil your dog's chances

- Stringing it up too tight on the lead will cause it to compensate by standing on tiptoe, which will make it knuckle over and its elbows come out. Some handlers prefer to place the forequarters by standing in front of the dog, lifting the feet off the ground together and lowering them into place, but this can cause the hindquarters to be overstretched, the forelegs being too far forward. It can also create a gap between the elbow and the brisket when viewed from the side.
- Placing the back legs too far beneath the dog or too far back will distort its frame; it will hunch its back to try to compensate for the discomfort, and also if the legs are placed too far back it will appear as if the dog has little turn of stifle.

- Holding the tail too high spoils its topline, too low has the same effect, giving the dog a lifeless look.

Timing

Timing is an important factor if the dog is to be seen at its best. Never have your dog at a disadvantage whilst in the ring. Do not relax, nor allow the dog to forget that it is in the show ring, and that you expect a lot of it. When you first come into the ring set the dog up, so that it knows why it is there; this steadies the dog as well as you. If you have to wait too long for the judge to walk down the line, let your dog relax by walking round you, then set it up again.

As you are waiting your turn to be gone over, make sure your dog is ready to go when the judge calls you up. Take your time setting your dog up correctly and do not fuss it.

A good judge will give you time to set your dog up so that its best points may be seen. A golden rule of showing is never take your eye off the judge.

HANDLING

Your ideal show career depends on how good a specimen your puppy develops into, but whatever happens you will need to learn how to show and handle the dog to the best advantage. There are very few dogs which cannot be taught to behave as they should. Anyone who does obedience training will have learnt very quickly that it is always the handler who has not learnt to teach the dog correctly, rather than the dog's inability to learn. So with this in mind, and irrespective of conformation, a dog well handled is always a treat to see.

An HPR should not be difficult to train. It is a gundog so it should be in its nature to want to please and work for you. The dog is usually very easy to train in basic obedience. Naturally as a youngster of three months you would not expect it to stand for long, or tolerate much formal teaching for that matter, but as it matures, with patience and firmness, you can expect a high degree of showing ability with the correct teaching. The dog should be perfectly capable of standing and moving in the show ring to a very high standard.

The handler's personality, feelings and skills will directly affect the way the dog behaves at a show. If you feel your dog cannot learn to stand still or move correctly, it is certainly not going to learn by itself. Give yourself confidence and some knowledge by watching good handlers, then try it. It is important to be patient with yourself and your dog. Of course you will make mistakes, but as long as you admit to them instead of blaming your dog no harm is done. When you show the dog, adopt the attitude that it is your pride and joy. It is difficult when the dog does not show as well as you know it can. But as you both become more and more accustomed to the performance you and your charge can enjoy the experience together. If you are able to keep your sense of humour at the same time, everyone will enjoy watching you. Never believe that you are the only one who has difficulties or that you are the only one who is nervous and tense as you stand in the ring – some are cleverer than others at covering up their feelings. Of course your dog will feel the tension but this can be put to good use, combined with the excitement and sense of occasion. Many, if not all, brilliant performers in other fields can give their best only when they are really keyed up. You can liken the day of the show to a performance in the theatre – months of hard rehearsing until the day arrives. The tension mounts, tempers quicken; come the moment, it can either be a complete flop or a resounding success. Whatever the outcome, if there is talent there it will come out sooner or later.

Teaching a puppy how to stand and move correctly, and learning ring manners is quite a task. You will need to be guided by the dog's temperament and stage of maturity as to how much you can expect. But from very early on, each day give the dog a few minutes of some sort of training. You can do this in your kitchen, hallway, or in the middle of the garden, park or field – in fact anywhere with a bit of space. Kneel down and stand the dog in front of you. It does not matter how it stands at first, just get it used to covering the ground, so that its legs are taking its weight equally. You can help the dog by holding its muzzle from underneath with your right hand. If it does not like that, steady the animal by holding its neck. Try running your left hand over and over its back to relax it. Talk to your dog and praise it so that it finds enjoyment. Then either place each back leg separately or put your hand between its back legs and lift its quarters off the ground, replacing them gently down again so that the dog is standing squarely on its four legs. Then hold the tail with the left hand. Of course it will not work at first – one end will go up, the other down – but it will come in time. You may get a surprise. The dog may do it perfectly well if you are firm. The golden rule is, always finish any lesson at any age on a note of success. If a lesson does not go well, take your dog back to an exercise you know it can do. If lessons always end in failure and tension and your displeasure is obvious, your HPR is not going to want to repeat that lesson, so you will have a stubborn dog on your hands.

If you feel you are losing your cool, leave your dog in peace or do something with it that you can both enjoy and leave the lesson for an other day. It needs to get used to being touched all over, so get into the habit of looking at its teeth regularly, inspecting its ears, inside its feet up, running your hands underneath and over its back, inside its back legs and, in the case of a male, over its scrotum. Get your dog used to every move you know the judge will need to make.

Once your puppy is used to its collar and lead you can introduce it to its show lead. There are many different makes and types on the market. Personally, I like a narrow leather slip lead that is not too long; leather is easy on the hands and it is strong enough to check an HPR if necessary. It is important that you find something that suits you and that you find comfortable. Keep the show lead just for show training and for shows, because a dog soon picks up the idea that its everyday lead means walks and that the other means using its brain as well as having fun with you.

You need to teach your puppy to trot correctly. At first it will be all over the place, but trot gently, encouraging the dog, talking to it, keeping its attention and teaching it to keep its head up, which it will do if you keep up an incessant chatter. When the dog does it right, take the lead off and let it leap and play, knowing it has pleased you. Then stop, put the lead back on again and trot, saying 'trot' so that it learns the word. Soon it learns that when the lead goes on, you mean business. As soon as you take it off, the dog knows it means fun and games. This way, it really does enjoy the job in hand. This will stand you in good stead throughout your dog's life. This is how you will get the very best out of an HPR. You must never forget to praise.

There are many different methods of showing the various breeds and it is an art to handle dogs well. The professional handler is there to display the dog to its full advantage. He will do this with such skill that it looks simple, but anyone who handles well knows it is not easy at all and takes much practice, time, patience and insight. It is said that a good handler can make a poor dog look good, or a bad handler a good one look poor. Maybe that is so, but if a dog is handled badly no judge can see enough to make his own mind up.

So the time will come when your dog is old enough for you to decide what method you will use, which manner of handling suits it best, taking into consideration that the freer and less cluttered up any dog looks, the more the judge likes it.

The free-standing method

This must be the ideal style. It can be seen in the Labrador ring to perfection. The dog stands alone, with the handler in front holding the lead loosely, a titbit at the ready. The dog stands stock still with its tail slowly swinging from side to side. A lovely sight, accentuating its excellent temperament and conformation.

If your dog has a calm, placid temperament, is extrovert and enjoys standing freely, it is well worth giving it a try. There is no doubt that it is very effective when it works.

To train your HPR to show this way takes time. Titbits, firmness and praise must be used as always. To start with, try standing in front of the dog with the lead loose, and titbits in your hand. Concentrate on the dog's eyes and say 'stand' (it does not matter how at this stage). If it sits, put the titbits away, go back to it, stand it using the word and run your hand along its back so that it begins to associate the hand movement with the word. When the dog feels steady enough, stand in front of it again and repeat the performance. If it stays for two seconds praise it and give it the food, but do not over-excite it. Stay calm, then try again and again and again. You can stand the dog correctly if you find it is getting the message and seems really steady. Then the fun begins. Practise each day and you will find that your dog will stand longer and longer, enjoying its sense of balance. Eventually you may find that you can count up to 100 (under your breath) without it moving. By that time I am sure you will have found that this method suits you both.

The drawbacks to this way of showing are numerous. If your dog has a lively and vivacious temperament it may not suit to have the handler stand so far away. Secondly, there is nothing like it for emphasising faults, such as bad feet or elbows, nor it is easy to adjust the stance of the dog if it moves. If the dog tends to tuck its tail the handler has no way of correcting it. If your dog is the fussy type the smell of food may over-excite it; on the other hand, some dogs are never tempted by a tid-bit once they are in the ring.

Topping and tailing

This way of showing a dog has exactly the opposite effect of the free-standing method. The advantages are that the dog is close to its owner which it likes. If it moves its feet or head they can be quickly corrected without the handler moving. The tail is held and it does not take so long to set the dog up.

To train your dog to show this way takes less time and patience than the free-standing method, but you need all your skill to prevent it from turning its head towards you, since you are practically eye to eye!

Stand your dog as you have taught it, holding its muzzle. Then kneel down on one knee, or two if you like, and support the dog's tail in the usual manner, allowing the lead to drop loosely round its neck.

The disadvantage is that the outline can be marred by the handler looking over the dog. If the dog does not like being held by the muzzle, it will either lean back away from your hand, which will shorten its neck, or it will lift its muzzle too high in the air, causing its back to hunch in protest. Thus it will not be correctly balanced. If you are over a certain age, struggling up and down on your knees will not do your lumbago any good either! I do not think this method is for a gundog breed, at least not the larger ones since they should have an independent aspect and should be allowed to stand as naturally as possible.

Free standing/topping and tailing

This is a compromise between the free-standing and topping and tailing methods. The handler stands, holding or supporting the muzzle or neck, or holding the lead up behind the ears and leaving the head entirely free. Meanwhile the tail is held in the correct position. The advantage of this method is that you are not restricted in any way, by either standing in front of the dog or kneeling down. You are free to shift your weight either towards the head or to the dog's rear. You can stand close or at arm's length. If your dog is really showing well that day, full of confidence and as steady as a rock, you can stand back, with the minimum of handling; on the other hand, if your dog has the fidgets, you can be close enough to put it right.

Many handlers like to use titbits – a bit of biscuit, meat or whatever the dog fancies best. If titbits are used, better to have them in your pocket out of the way so that your dog can smell them. If you hold them out, the dog either leaps for them or just manages to be chewing a piece as the judge approaches to look at its teeth!

Whichever method is chosen and I suspect we all use a bit of each, what is essential is that we are decisive so that the dog can understand what we are asking. Some dogs have more grey matter than others, but they cannot learn to show by themselves.

When practising, try standing your HPR before a full-length mirror, sideways and frontways (this is what the judge sees). It can be quite a shock. You think your dog is set up just right, but you look in the mirror and everything is wrong! A friend is just as useful as a mirror, if not more so, for you can discuss, criticise, take it in turns to look at each other's dogs. The work and anticipation is almost more fun than the day itself.

TYPES OF DOG SHOW

Exemption shows

Most people's introduction to showing comes from attending the small dog shows which are often held in conjunction with local fêtes and agricultural shows. These shows are held under the jurisdiction of the Kennel Club and are known as exemption shows. Only four pedigree classes are allowed. These usually come under class headings such as sporting, non-sporting, working and utility. Other classes are the novelty classes such as best short-haired dog, dog with the 'waggiest tail', dog with the prettiest face and so on. After all the novelty classes have been judged, the class winners compete for the best in show title. Wins at exemption shows do not count towards any titles such as junior warrant.

Matches

Matches are often held by 'ringcraft' clubs. They involve pedigree dogs only. Once again they are held under Kennel Club rules, although clubs do not need to obtain permission. An outsider is often called in to judge. Matches are really just social affairs which give good grounding in ring behaviour.

Sanction shows

These are licensed by the Kennel Club and are subject to more rules and regulations. A schedule has to be issued and the number of classes is limited.

Limit shows

These are slightly more advanced than sanction shows. There must be a minimum of 21 classes if more than one breed is scheduled or, if just one breed, a minimum of 13 classes. Any dog which has won a challenge certificate is not eligible to be shown at the foregoing types of show.

Open shows

These can have any number of classes and are open to all types of pedigree dog which are registered with the Kennel Club.

Championship shows

These are the shows at which the much sought after challenge certificates are awarded. These shows cater for nearly every type of pedigree dog found in Britain. They are held all over the country; winning a class at a championship show means that one can enter for Crufts.

Crufts

To enter Crufts – this world-famous show – one first must qualify a dog at a championship show. A show champion or champion dog can be shown at Crufts without having to qualify as it has already proved its quality.

Definition of classes

Minor puppy   For dogs of six and not exceeding nine calendar months of age on the day of the show.

Puppy   For dogs of six and not exceeding twelve calendar months of age on the day of the show.

Junior   For dogs of six and not exceeding eighteen calendar months of age on the day of the show.

Special yearling   For dogs of six months and not exceeding two years of age on the day of the show.

Maiden   For dogs which have not won a challenge certificate or a first prize at an open or championship show (puppy, special puppy, minor and special minor puppy classes excepted).

Novice   For dogs which have not won a challenge certificate or three or more first prizes at open or championship shows (puppy, special puppy, minor and special minor puppy classes excepted).

Undergraduate   For dogs which have not won a challenge certificate or three or more first prizes at championship shows (puppy, special puppy, minor and special minor puppy classes excepted).

Graduate   For dogs which have not won a challenge certificate or four or more first prizes at championship shows in graduate, post graduate, minor limit, mid limit and open classes whether restricted or not.

Post graduate   For dogs which have not won a challenge certificate or five or more first prizes at championship shows in post graduate, minor limit, mid limit, limit and open classes whether restricted or not.

Limit   For dogs which have not won three challenge certificates under three different judges or seven or more first prizes in all at championship shows in limit and open classes, confined to the breed, whether restricted or not, at shows where challenge certificates were offered in the breed.

Open	For all dogs of the breeds for which the class is provided and eligible for entry at the show.
Special open	As for open classes except that it is restricted as to weight, height, colour or to members of an association.
Field trial	For dogs which have won prizes, awards of honour, diplomas of merit or certificates of merit in actual competition at a field trial held under Kennel Club or Irish Kennel Club field trial rules and regulations.
Special beginners	For dogs and bitches shown by an exhibitor whose dogs have never won a challenge certificate in the breed. (Note: it is the exhibitor who has to qualify *not* the dog.)
Brace	For two exhibits (either sex or mixed) of one breed belonging to the same exhibitor, each exhibit having been entered in some class other than brace or team.
Team	For three exhibits (either sex or mixed) of one breed belonging to the same exhibitor, each exhibit having been entered in some class other than brace or team.
Veteran	For dogs of seven years of age and over on the day of the show.

Special regulations

When a dog is not fully registered at the British Kennel Club there are certain letters which must be placed after the dog's name on the entry form to indicate that permission has been applied for but that the owner has not yet received confirmation from the Kennel Club. These are as follows:

NAF – Name Applied For
TAF – Transfer Applied For
ARAF – Active Register Applied For

Junior warrant

How do you gain a junior warrant? If your puppy turns out to be a good one and you discover that every time you show it you come out of the ring with a red card in your hand, it may be worthwhile trying to gain a junior warrant. This is a special award offered by the Kennel Club for puppies which have gained 25 points from the age of six months up to eighteen months. Three points can be acquired by any first prize won in a breed class at a championship show. At a championship show without challenge certificates for the breed or open shows, a first prize counts as one point.

On attaining the 25 points the certificate has to be applied for. The Kennel Club does not automatically send it, as it does the challenge certificate. Unfortunately there is no way of recognising a dog which has won its junior warrant either; there are no letters before its name indicating this award. Even so, it is well worth notching up those wins. It will be a strong indication that the puppy may gain show champion status later on, although it is not always so.

10
WORKING TESTS

John Wagstaff

For many more years than I care to remember I have been deeply embroiled with working tests, as an organiser, judge and individual handler. For the novice trainer these tests provide the perfect means to demonstrate varying degrees of training ability on behalf of dog and handler. Some handlers will treat working tests as an initial step towards field trials, whilst for others they may be an end in themselves. Above all, working tests are fun and should be treated as such, though that is not to suggest that they should be entered lightly or without sufficient thought. It is obviously essential that your HPR should have received and absorbed its basic training before any consideration is given to entering a working test.

Tests are held throughout the country and all the year round, thus giving the owner every opportunity to achieve a reasonable standard with his or her dog. Obviously there are degrees of proficiency and if you and your dog become sufficiently accomplished you may be asked to represent your breed club at an invitation working test at a country fair. These tests are run as demonstration events to display to the public the capabilities of the several HPR breeds. They are usually extremely well organised and frequently watched by hundreds of spectators. One of the more ambitious branches of the German Short-haired Pointer Club is the South Eastern County Branch which organises the largest HPR working test. This is an annual event with a conformation show and gundog scurry as well. It has catered for over a hundred entries, and is very popular as part of the proceeds go to the German short-haired pointer rescue fund.

If you are a new owner or are thinking of acquiring one of the HPR breeds, you will quickly appreciate the benefits to be gained by joining one or more of the breed clubs. You will receive newsletters with information on club and branch activities, including training classes.

When you receive your working test entry form you will find details of the venue, date and time of the test. You may also be given additional information about what will be required of your dog in the puppy and novice classes, so that you will have some idea of what to expect on the day. The form has to be completed and returned by a certain date, which will be clearly stated, along with the entry fee. Entry fees are usually calculated per class entered. Information required on the form is the breed, age and sex of your dog, plus details of the specific class or classes in which you wish the animal to compete. You will also be required to supply two 1 lb standard training dummies with your name clearly marked on each. These will be returned to you at the end of the day.

On the day of the working test no bitches in heat will be allowed on the ground and all dogs must be fully vaccinated. Dogs must also be kept on leads at all times except when under running orders or in a designated exercise area. The lead rule must be adhered to at all times as the organisers cannot be held responsible for any damage to you or your dog.

CLASSES OF WORKING TEST

All dogs are to be over six months of age on the day of the test. There are normally three classes at a working test, comprising puppy, novice and open. Some of the HPR clubs have now introduced a new class, known as the graduate class. This, in my opinion, is a very wise move as many handlers were finding the transition from novice to open too large a step.

The puppy class is open to dogs from 6 months to 18 months. A dog falling into this category can continue to run in puppy classes regardless of the number of times it may win. The novice class is open to all dogs that have not won a novice, graduate or open test or been placed in a field trial. The open test is for all dogs of an open standard, irrespective of whether they have been placed in a field trial.

Typical tests in all four classes might comprise the following. In the puppy class you could have heel work through a slalom of canes, sit and stay with recall to order, a seen retrieve to order and a short retrieve from water. The novice test could consist of a seen retrieve over a jump, a split retrieve to order, a long memory retrieve and a seen retrieve from water. In the open test, depending on the ground available, one might have hunting and pointing of caged game and various retrieves of cold game, with the distraction of a bolting rabbit or a dummy launcher while the dog is retrieving. This might be followed by a blind retrieve across water. The graduate test would be very similar to the open test, but the retrieving test would be considerably less difficult.

BEHIND THE SCENES

A great many people who participate have no conception of the amount of work, time and effort involved in the setting up of a working test. Only if something goes wrong do they complain, seldom taking the trouble to appreciate that a smooth-running test does not just happen – it takes a vast amount of planning.

Firstly a suitable date has to be chosen which does not clash with any other working test dates in the area. Then the selected judges have to be notified in sufficient time for them to confirm that they will be available. Normally judges would be asked to choose their own stewards, although this can be arranged by the club if they are unable to do so. Many judges coerce their partners into this task!

Entry forms have to be printed and sent sufficiently early to ensure a good attendance, while trophies and rosettes also have to be ordered. The perpetual trophies have to be reclaimed and the current holders given sufficient notice. There is nothing more embarrassing than having to tell the winner of an annual trophy that the previous winner has not yet returned it.

The selection of the ground on which the test is to be run has to be given very careful consideration. Certain factors have to be taken into account. Reasonable access to the ground is essential, and this applies in particular to a new ground as one can guarantee that someone, somehow, despite careful instructions, will manage to get lost. Even if the same venue is used annually the actual ground must be visited to ensure that it has not been altered due, perhaps, to crop rotation. I always draw a plan of the area so that I know exactly where the different classes will be run.

The most level ground at the venue should be used for car-parking and also for the administration area. Ideally, the level ground is also used for the puppy test, whilst ground with contours and hedgerows, ditches and rough cover will be retained for the novice and open tests. If the ground lacks natural cover for the concealment of dummy placers and throwers it is essential that hides are constructed. There is nothing more likely to deter a young dog than someone trying to hide in 6 inches of wet grass! When water is available checks must be made to discover a suitable gradual entry point. This can be used by the dogs in all classes at different times during the day. On land fresh ground should be used whenever possible.

For each class a team of two competent helpers is needed to throw and place the dummies. This enables one to be relieved when necessary as this can be a long and tedious job. All dummy throwers must be upwind from the area from which the dog is expected to retrieve and a stout plastic bag should be supplied in which to keep the dummies or cold game so that a dog cannot take the scent of a pile of dummies in an exposed area or be distracted by trying to retrieve them. Dummy throwers have the most important task at a working test. They must be fully briefed so that they understand that seen retrieves must be thrown only when a shot is fired or the judge indicates, and should be clearly outlined against the skyline. If the dummies or cold game are to be placed for blind retrieves, care must be taken to ensure that they are placed in the same spot, thus giving each dog an equal chance.

It is, of course, not just one person who organises and ensures the smooth running of a working test, but a host of volunteers all working together and equally hard. It takes several workers actually to prepare the venue for a working test. Hides have to be placed in strategic sites if natural cover is not available, whilst jumps may also have to be built. Administrators are required on the day, whilst refreshments are usually available and, of course, have to be served. This task is often undertaken by women members of the club; they, too, are often responsible for the administrative side, including serving the judges' lunches and running a raffle.

An overall administrator usually supervises and advises on all the above aspects of the day. This is often the club chairman; amongst his or her duties will be to greet the judges, liaise with spectators who may include locals intrigued by the activity, oversee the setting up of all the tests, and designate all the many other jobs. Most of the construction work will have been done the day before the test, apart from the erecting of signs directing competitors. If set out the night before these may well be moved by the malicious or stupid.

If the area in which the test takes place has sufficient ground for a hunting test, you will require at least two or three gamebirds of any description. Strong cages should be used, each not much larger than the bird it contains. My 'pointing' cages are constructed from small-gauge rolled mesh in a roof-top design with stout pegs to hold it down. It should be just large enough to accommodate the bird so that it will crouch tight, just as it would under normal field circumstances when threatened by the presence of a dog.

Ideally, cages should be placed so that there is room for the dog to approach from any angle. This is essential in order to allow for any change in wind direction which may occur. The caged game should be put out as early as possible on the day, picked up as soon as the pointing test is over and then transferred to a larger cage for transportation.

THE WORKING TEST

On the day of the test you owe it to yourself and your dog to arrive in plenty of time. It is sensible to prepare all that you require the night before, making sure you have water and a bowl, spare leads, whistles and, for yourself, warm and waterproof clothing if the weather looks doubtful. A first-aid kit should also feature in the list.

When you arrive check into the administration area and collect your running number(s) for the day. The exercise area will usually be signposted and it is obviously sensible to let your dog have a few moments' relaxation here after the journey, followed by a few basic commands to put it in the right frame of mind. During the course of the day you may find that your dog, whilst waiting for its turn to compete, is beginning to tire, so try and keep it as fresh as possible by returning as often as necessary to the exercise area.

Try to relax yourself, otherwise your dog will sense the tension and may react accordingly with a spoiled performance. No one can foresee what will happen on the day and no amount of worrying will alter the outcome. If you are uncertain of anything ask someone; everyone is a beginner once, and gundog folk are only too willing to share their knowledge and point you in the right direction. Above all, remember that both of you are there to have a good time.

At the start of the test the chairman will call all the competitors together and introduce them to the various judges and stewards of each class. The designated areas for the several classes will be explained. If you are running more than one dog in different classes the stewards for each class should be notified so that, if your number is called and you are not present, this can be allowed for to enable you to run later. If you decide, at any stage, to withdraw your dog from the competition, it is common courtesy to advise the steward of the class or classes for which you were entered.

Remember that at a designated time there will be a break for lunch so, even if you have not completed your run when the break commences, proceedings will start exactly where they left off when the competition recommences.

During the competition judges will be looking for certain specific points. In the puppy class I always note whether there is a harmony between the handler and dog. I like to see a handler really trying to help and encourage his or her dog, even if this means resorting to soothing verbal directions. Above all I like to see a happy and willing puppy.

In the open and novice classes the judge will be looking for total steadiness to shot and good marking in retrieves, with competent, quiet handling on the hunting and pointing test. He will want to see effective ground coverage with a strong indication and point to the scent of the caged game. Noisy and ineffective handling will be marked down, and the judge will also take note of the dog's response to the handler. In the water test a bold entrance is sought, with strong swimming and clean delivery of the dummy on the retrieve. General keenness and alertness are looked for at all times.

At the end of the day, hopefully you will find yourself waiting, along with the other competitors, for the final scores to be added and the results announced. This can take some time as obviously the results must be accurate and some tests may take longer to complete than others. Finally the results will be given and the prizes awarded. The judges will give their summing up, from which useful hints and advice can be gleaned. You may also get the opportunity to speak to a judge and discuss your run. Try to thank the secretary and organiser for an enjoyable day; such small courtesies mean a great deal.

I enjoy all aspects of working tests as they provide me with the opportunity to work and keep my dog fit throughout the year, whilst also enabling me to make new friends and watch good dogs working. I hope that working tests will continue to flourish and be organised by individual branch groups and clubs for years to come, for in this way not only is a great deal of pleasure derived but a certain degree of financial independence is gained.

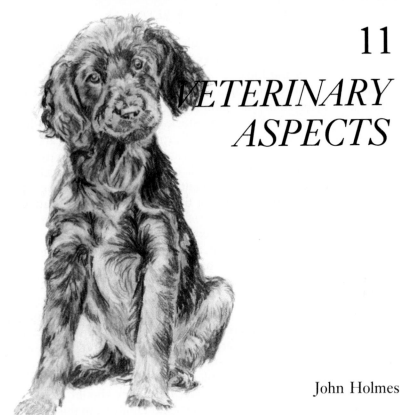

11
VETERINARY ASPECTS

John Holmes

CHOOSING A PUPPY

The reasons why you should or should not choose an HPR puppy have already been considered elsewhere in this book. As they are specialist breeds of dog chosen for their all-round abilities, it is important, when you set out to choose a pup, that you should know roughly what you are looking for and the reasons for your choice. You will have enough difficulties ahead of you with training and rearing without making obvious mistakes in the first place. You can try to ensure that you do not buy a nervous puppy with a reasonable chance of success.

Try to keep an open mind when you go to inspect a litter of puppies. If possible ask to see the stud dog and see whether he is nervous, recessive or responsive to commands when running free or in a pen. If practical, do the same with the bitch. If signs of apprehension, nervousness or aggression are shown then these points may appear in the litter of pups from which you are trying to choose. There could be hereditary factors involved. Look also at the conformation of both parents to see if their structure accords with the breed standards given at the start of the chapters on individual HPR breeds.

At the same time ask for details about both dog and bitch to ascertain whether they have been certified free of hereditary diseases affecting the eyes and hips.

There is a joint scheme approved by the Kennel Club and British Veterinary Association and administered by specialised veterinary surgeons to try to clear breeding stock of hereditary eye conditions such as retinal atrophy and cataract. Certified official forms are issued and should be inspected. There is a similar scheme for hip dysplasia, which causes dogs to have a weak back end as they develop. All breeding stock should be X-rayed and a certificate given. The hip X-ray is scored by a panel of experts, the lower numbers indicating the better-quality hips. Alas, there are still many breeders who ignore these schemes – or prevaricate. I consider such attitudes irresponsible towards the future wellbeing of the various breeds. I would avoid choosing a pup from a litter of unexamined parentage.

By far the most important factor in your search for temperament should be how, and where, the pups are reared. Puppies reared in a kennel and run well away from house and humans have a tendency to bark and be nervous. Perhaps they are only seen two or three times daily at feeding times. They are more difficult to handle and train as they develop because they have not been closely associated with humans from an early age. Puppies are able to hear, smell, feel and sense things from at least seven days old. They should be handled sensibly and frequently by their owners and family from this early age. Many scientific experiments have shown that the most suitable age for puppies to be 'imprinted' by human influence is between three to five weeks old. From eight to ten weeks old they can still be influenced, but to a declining degree. If a puppy has not been influenced and imprinted by 10 weeks, the chances are that it will be nervous to a greater or lesser degree. No amount of schooling, training, kindness or affection in later development will ever completely make up for lack of influence at an early age.

The best time first to inspect your puppy is at around five weeks old. You can then observe whether it is bold or recessive or barks nervously. Hopefully it will have a friendly wag of its tail for you and come forward to inspect you in a curious, interested way. It should not run away when you stoop down to pick it up. It should rest on the palm of your hand in a confident manner, inspecting you and your clothing with interested curiosity, but without any frozen stillness or nervous rigidity. After fondling when you place it on the ground it should continue inspection of your shoes and clothing in a buoyant manner. It may even try to eat them! Beware of the puppy that at this stage runs back into the kennel and hides from you.

Much has been written on the merits and demerits of owning a dog or a bitch. It has been my experience as a vet, and a trainer of HPRs, that dogs tend to mature at a later age than bitches. They are slower at learning and tend to become distracted more easily during their 'puberty' development. They often try to develop their 'top dog' personality and will initially need more positive handling to make sure that their owner/handler stays as top dog or pack leader. They are also more easily distracted in the field by the scent of other dogs or bitches. Bitches, on the other hand, develop earlier and more easily. They seem to relate to their owner/handler more positively than a dog and are keen to please. But they also come into season twice a year, which may mean loss of working time. The choice of sex is an individual one and there are no fixed rules.

Your puppy at eight weeks old should look fit, well muscled and bouncy. If you decide to buy it, it would be advisable to tell the breeder that if you are purchasing it only on condition that it passes your vet's inspection within the next seven days. This puts the law on your side and should enable you to return the pup within that period if a major fault is found. Take note of its present diet and feeding regime.

FEEDING AND EARLY MANAGEMENT

Much has been written on the feeding of dogs and their requirements. Most of it seems to me to be more statistical than practical, based on manufacturers' recommendations rather than the true needs of the animal.

Primaevally, the dog was a carnivore. It obtained the bulk of its diet by killing herbivores and rodents, feeding on large volumes of meat and fat and chewing bones, all of which it digested adequately. Part of its meat intake was the intestines of its kill – very often the large stomach of ruminants was selected first. From all these facts we can safely say that provided food (i.e. game) was available, the dog was well maintained and fit from a nutritional aspect. Animal protein and fat were provided. Bones gave minerals, vitamins and trace elements – they also provided large quantities of roughage, an essential and much-neglected part of the modern dog's diet. The practical aspects of an essential diet for puppies and adult dogs can, therefore, be simplified by referring to the preceding observations. It can be elaborated as common sense, age and practicality dictate.

A diet for your puppy should consist of animal proteins and fats fed three or four times daily at eight weeks old. Carbohydrates and milk are not essential. Give it 10 minutes only to clear up its food, then remove it until the next meal. If a feeding time is not greeted with enthusiasm, cut it out and feed two or three meals daily. There is a great deal of individual variation here. What is certain is that a pup will eat what it requires provided the correct food is available.

Let us consider in more detail the essentials of a practical diet.

Proteins

These should consist of animal protein – meats, fish, eggs, cheese, pet mince from the butcher or pet shop and raw green tripe. Various 'meat rolls' or 'brawns' contain good quality proteins. They can be shelf-stored for several months. Most of the 'complete' dog-foods contain large quantities of vegetable protein such as soya, peas, beans and lentils. They may be adequate but your pup deserves better. Either add animal protein to them or replace with animal proteins two or three times weekly. Raw meat is preferable to cooked. Pork can cause problems with parasites and digestive upsets – do not feed it raw or cooked. Offal (heart, liver, kidneys) can cause diarrhoea if fed in quantity. Many tinned foods are far too concentrated. My experience has led me to believe them responsible for a large proportion of cases of gastro-enteritis in large dogs. I do not recommend them. A variety of protein foods 'educates' the normal bowel flora to accept different types of protein without causing stomach or intestinal upsets.

Fats

Dogs are able to digest up to half their dietary input as fat, provided they eat adequate roughage. Fat is in green tripe, pet mince and suet. Pork or pork fat cause vomiting and distress. Margarine and vegetable oils can be substituted for animal fats but the animal fats are preferable.

Carbohydrates

Biscuit meals etc. are a non-essential part of diet. Roughly speaking, the larger the dog the more likely it is to utilise additional biscuit meal or biscuit. Almost any brand will do.

Fibre

A much-neglected part of diets for dogs, fibre is responsible for the expansion and correct functioning of the digestive tract. Wild dogs naturally eat hide, gristle and bones for their roughage. We can artificially provide bran of all sorts or proprietary human breakfast foods. As a general rule between a quarter and a half of the diet's daily volume should be roughage.

Bones

Bones are an essential part of diet for all dogs. Raw rib bones, blade bones and neck bones of beef (or lamb) should be fed at least once weekly. No cooked bones, chicken bones or pork bones of any sort should be fed at all. Marrow bones contain overrich marrow which should be scraped out and fed mixed with the next few meals. Bone chewing and digesting creates roughage and encourages a healthy mouth, gums and teeth. Regular bone feeding prevents tartar formation over the years. Bones may cause fights between adult or growing dogs, so feed them individually.

Trace elements, minerals and vitamins
Vitamin B complex is contained naturally in raw meat; vitamins A and D in raw bones, bone marrow and vegetable oils. Calcium is in bones in absorbable form and also in milk. Trace elements are in bones (and the fermenting vegetables in green tripe); an occasional pinch of seaweed powder adds the main essential minerals. Additives are mostly unnecessary and will be excreted by the dog. If they make you feel better on behalf of your dog, add them with caution. I only give them to my dogs in high-stress situations.

Fluids
Water should be freely available at all times. Dogs love drinking from puddles, ditches and foul green fishponds without coming to any harm. Milk is a food and excess of it suppresses normal appetite; give small quantities of milk daily or infrequently.

Vegetables and table scraps
Cooked vegetables add little to diet. Table scraps can be added as roughage. Sweet biscuits, potatoes, puddings, etc. add too much carbohydrate. They may also put the dog off its normal food.

Baby foods
Concentrated and predigested baby foods are unnecessary and unwise after eight weeks old. They are too easily absorbed and lack roughage. They promote a fat belly and a scurvy coat.

Quantities
As a rough guide feed approximately 1 oz protein for every 2 lbs bodyweight daily. Active puppies may need twice this quantity. Add to it approximately half this amount by volume of wholemeal biscuit or 'complete' dog food. Be prepared to vary quantities according to the animal's condition.

Overweight
Do not worry about a high-protein-fed puppy until it is almost a year old. If you are uncertain of its condition, seek professional advice.

Changes of diet
These should be made gradually over a 48-hour period. Sudden changes of protein may cause diarrhoea or sickness. Your puppy will find enough problems by itself in this direction without you adding to them!

To be more specific, my HPR puppies get 1–2 lbs of raw green tripe daily, the odd cooked egg and some fish mixed with roughage. Bones are regularly available. An occasional saucer of milk is given. They are fast growing, glossy coated, plump and active. I do very little else of a dietary nature for them. They are fed regularly. On a high-animal-protein diet they soon go to two meals a day, then down to one at six to eight months old. I make great allowance for individual variations with quantitites. My dogs are all very fit and develop normally and rapidly.

As the puppy grows, its food intake maintains at roughly the same quantities. In the early stages food is required for normal rapid bodily growth and development. After eight to ten months of age the growth rate is almost complete but the larger, more adult frame requires more for maintenance and equilibrium.

Exercise is important. The young puppy eats, plays and sleeps. If it is kept indoors it needs letting out frequently to urinate and defecate. It prefers to carry out these functions on grass but a back yard will suffice. Newspaper placed by the back door encourages urination there until the puppy is old enough to ask to go out or until you recognise its 'anxious' signs. If you have a garden, walk round with it at least every two hours. If kept in a kennel and run, most puppies naturally use the yard area for these purposes. I prefer to keep mine in the house, where I get to know their characters better and vice versa.

An eight-week-old puppy should have been wormed for round-worms at least three times before you get it. It is advisable to worm with a proprietary wormer regularly every month until the age of six months, followed by routine six-monthly worming. Your vet can advise you on worming when he inspects the pup soon after purchase and begins immunisation against the major dog diseases at about eight weeks old. These diseases are as follows.

Hard pad and distemper
This is a viral disease causing discharging eyes, diarrhoea and vomiting, ultimately affecting the brain and causing fits. There is no certain cure. Immunisation is safe and prevents it adequately.

Parvo virus
Parvo virus is a newer disease, mostly of puppies, causing sudden acute diarrhoea and vomiting and great dullness. It is mostly fatal. Modern vaccines adequately prevent it.

Leptospirosis

There are two bacterial varieties of this, both affecting liver and kidneys. The very acute forms cause jaundice and are mostly fatal. The chronic forms work insidiously on the kidneys and may lead to premature death at middle age; they can be caught from rats. Immunisation prevents the acute symptoms. (The disease can be cured if recognised in time).

Hepatitis

Hepatitis is a virus liver infection with similar symptoms and results to leptospirosis. Immunisation in puppies is effective.

Kennel cough

This viral infection is rarely a problem for individual owners and usually clears with veterinary attention.

Effective immunisation is necessary against all these diseases. A booster injection against them all is currently required annually. Your canine companion is then protected as far as possible against infectious diseases. With a good diet it should then stay healthy and fit.

Exercise is important in maintaining this fitness. To a large extent the more a dog or bitch uses its muscle, the better it develops. I exercise all puppies that I own from eight to twelve weeks old with the bigger adult dogs in a confined space. After twelve weeks, when their immunisation against the above diseases is complete, I take them out with the older dogs. The pups run behind the others and take their place in the pack. They run into water, go in the sea and hunt out the dunes and downs. They come back tired and relaxed and then have what time they want to sleep it off. They learn pack laws and pack discipline, and to eat, sleep and rest well. They also learn the training commands by repetition and example from the adult dogs. Their minds and bodies develop. They lose their puppy fat and develop muscle and sinew as they grow. All this is important from the point of view of physical and mental development through to adulthood.

VETERINARY MEDICAL NOTES

Parasites

Roundworms

The main roundworms found in the dog are *Toxocara canis*, *Toxascaris leonina* and *Toxocara cati*. The most significant one is *Toxocara canis*. It is also the most common. Treatment for this roundworm is also effective against the other two. Prevention of *Toxocara canis* is most important for puppies, where it can cause fatal infestations. In its larval forms it can, on rare occasions when it gains access to the human body, locate behind the eye and cause blindness.

Puppies are usually infected prenatally from encapsulated larvae in the dam's muscles. These are released into the dam's bloodstream under the influence of the hormones of pregnancy during about the last third of pregnancy. They obtain access to the foetus via its uterine blood supply. They go through a dormant stage until the pups are born, after which they develop finally in the puppy's intestine where they exist in large numbers from two weeks of age onwards. From then on they excrete huge quantitites of fertile eggs to the exterior via the faeces. The bitch can (and does) reinfest herself as she cleans up the pups. The pups naturally reinfest themselves by close contact. This process can repeat itself until well after the pups are weaned.

The symptoms caused in puppies can range from sudden death, with a large 'ball' of worms found in the intestine at post-mortem, to lack of thriving, poor condition and pot-belly. These can occur, as we have seen, from two weeks of age onwards. It is important, therefore, to enquire at eight weeks whether your puppy has been wormed at weekly intervals from three weeks of age onwards. Take advice on the subject from your vet at the eight-week-old inspection.

Fortunately, the adult and immature stages of *Toxocara canis* respond to correct therapy. Piperazine compounds are commonly and effectively used. They can be obtained from vet surgeries or pet shops. Follow the manufacturer's instructions for usage and dosage. If you are in doubt about the worm status of your pup, worm it regularly every two weeks for four consecutive wormings. If you cannot guess the weight of the animal overdose it. It is almost impossible to do any harm with the Piperazine compounds. They are best given crushed and dispersed with the food at a meal time.

Worms appear (in the faeces) up to 48 hours after treatment. They vary in size, looking roughly like a large garden worm but white in colour. Faeces containing worms, or otherwise, when passed near the house should be disposed of by burning or with antiseptic in a 'dog loo'. If you think worms are continuing to pass from your pup, consult your vet and have a faeces sample tested.

If you have a concrete run for your dog, it is advisable to scrub it down monthly with hot washing soda, followed by antiseptic. This tends to break down any encapsulated eggs of *Toxocara canis* and allows the sun and antiseptic to kill them.

Tapeworms

In Britain the main tapeworms are *Dipylidium caninum* and the *Taenia* species. Tapeworms all have a second host in their lifecycle and cannot be transmitted by direct contact. They are not as important as the roundworm but may on occasions cause unthriftiness, bowel upset or even fits. *Dipylidium caninum* has the flea as a secondary host and the dog reinfests itself by killing and ingesting infested fleas. *Taenia* species have rabbits, rats and mice as their secondary host and infest dogs who eat carrion – a favourite pastime of HPRs in the country!

The main sign of tapeworms is the appearance of shiny white segments in the rectal area and surrounding hairs. They measure 1–2 cm in length and expand and contract very slowly. When dried they stick to the hairs and look like rice grains. These are the segments that have been shed from a long adult ribbon or tape in your animal's intestine. There they may be well over a metre in length!

The most effective treatments are bought from your veterinary surgeon, who will advise on treatment for fleas at the same time.

Skin parasites
Of the main skin parasites – fleas, ticks, lice, ear mites and mange mites – the most common on the dog's skin is the flea. It is small, dark brown and fast moving when disturbed. It leaves behind 'flea dirts', which are small, dark, granular and about the size of a pin head. If placed on white paper and wetted the dirts show a red/brown blood colour. This is because fleas are parasitic and suck blood from your dog's skin. They can occur singly (for a while) or in hordes! They mostly cause continuous irritation and bald patches. They are the number one suspect in all summer eczema cases because they breed rapidly in warm conditions. Central heating is a bonus for them. They complete their lifecycle in dust and dirt and can stay under your carpets for up to two years. They can also be passed from dog to cat and vice versa, spreading tapeworms as they go. All in all, a most important parasite that should be thoroughly and systematically eradicated.

Treatment is basically in three parts. The fleas should first be removed from the dog with washes, powders and sprays. Your dog may then need professional skills to desensitise its skin from the acute allergic state caused by the fleas and any subsequent secondary infection. Finally, a proprietary preparation can be bought from vet surgeons or some pet shops to spray your room or rooms and carpet edges to kill off the parasites underneath. This usually lasts for three months at least and is very effective.

If you think your house is infested with fleas you can use the above control methods or consult the health department of your local council, which will fumigate your house for you. If the infestation reaches sufficient proportions, the fleas will certainly attack you and your family.

Ticks are parasites essentially of sheep, but they will appear on dogs' skins anywhere within 3 kilometres of where sheep are kept, particularly on grouse moors. They vary in colour from dark brown to grey. Their size varies from 2 mm to 2 cm. They suck blood, cause intense irritation and leave an infected or thickened area on the skin for several weeks after they have gone. They can transmit infections to the dog in the process of sucking blood. They cannot be prevented but can be killed by applying methylated spirit, flea spray or insecticidal shampoo, or by simply applying oil – vegetable or mineral – which blocks the air pores. If they have not dropped off within 30 minutes, pull them off.

Lice are not as common as they used to be. They mostly occur on long-coated dogs. The parasites are grey in colour and about the size of a flea, but move slowly across the skin when disturbed – like tiny crabs! They like warmth and can occur in large numbers. They are caught by contact with other infested dogs. The lice eggs, or 'nits', are attached obliquely, singly or in large numbers, to the hairs. Lice are blood suckers which live on the skin and cause intense irritation and a poor, dull coat. Modern insecticidal shampoos used at weekly intervals for three weeks cure the dog of these parasites.

Ear mites are minute parasites of the ears of dogs and cats, and are transmitted by close contact with other dogs or cats. They can be seen with a special magnifying instrument. The inflammation that arises from them allows secondary bacteria to invade, causing both acute and chronic ear problems. Ear mites are easily killed off as their lifecycle appears to be carried out only in the ears of dogs or cats. Apply ear drops for three days to kill them off, followed by twice-weekly application for three weeks to prevent any eggs from hatching and causing further problems. Reinfestation can come only by direct contact with an infested animal – not out of fresh air – so treat all dogs and cats in your menage. Ear mites are not known to be transmitted to human beings.

Mange mites are microscopic parasites living in the skin of dogs. There are basically two different varieties of mites, causing similar symptoms. Mixed infestations can occur. They cause skin irritation and thickening, especially under the belly, under the forearms and around the eyes, ears and muzzle. Invasion of the skin is thought to occur at birth and symptoms arise following stress, e.g. during teething, puberty or after road accidents. If caught in the early stages, specialised treatment can cure the vast majority of cases. This is positively a task for professional guidance, so consult your veterinary surgeon as soon as any skin symptoms arise.

Insurance and general injuries

Before discussing injuries and general medical problems, it is relevant here to say that there are now several insurance companies which specialise in the insurance of dogs against third-party risks and veterinary fees. The unfortunate occurrence of a road accident can lead to many hundreds of pounds in veterinary fees, followed by many thousands in third-party claims! Insurance also allows your veterinary surgeon to carry out all procedures he or she considers necessary to ensure the continued wellbeing of your animal without being inhibited professionally by the thought of the expense. I consider fully comprehensive dog insurance very cheap and an essential factor in the animal's care. It should be looked on as a form of private health insurance. If you are uncertain how to obtain insurance for your pet, your vet will be able to advise you at your eight-week-old inspection.

General notes on injuries

This is not the place to give detailed notes on major injuries such as fractures. I shall leave this to the specialised knowledge of the veterinary surgeon, who will guide you according to the individual requirements of the injury. The following words are intended to be a guide to the practical treatment by the dog owner of some of the routine problems encountered in everyday HPR life.

Minor injuries can include small cuts and abrasions. It is useful to check the dog after each exercise to find out what, if any, injuries have occurred. Some of the HPR breeds are very forceful in pushing their way through cover and tend to make the skin around the muzzle and eyes bare. This also will occur when working in wet farm crops such as kale or roots, or even in wet heather. I always bathe these injuries several times daily in a weak solution of proprietary hypochlorite used for sterilising nappies. Roughly a teaspoon to a cupful of water is an adequate dilution. It keeps off extraneous bacteria and promotes clean healing. It can be followed by bathing with a solution of Hypercal. This is a mixture of hypericum and calendula. It can be obtained from health food stores or homeopathic chemists. Dilute as per instructions or as for hypochlorite. When applied it seems to stimulate rapid healing. I find wound powders clog up the area and encourage the dog to positive licking to remove them. Antibiotics are unnecessary in the first place. If thorns are found anywhere in the skin remove them and proceed as previously. Eye injuries need careful observation. If they have not cleared up after 24 hours of simple treatment, consult professional advice. Ticks have been dealt with in the parasite section.

For more severe injuries, I always carry with me a pocket first-aid kit, consisting of: one pack of non-stick dressing; two open-weave bandages; two self-adhesive bandages; and one small bottle of dilute hypochlorite. These can all be obtained from a chemist and with a little practice can be applied to cut feet and legs to prevent initial haemorrhages. The blood loss from a cut pad can be quite alarming and should be stemmed as soon as possible prior to attending a veterinary surgery. If you can stop the haemorrhage with bandages and keep calm enough to telephone the clinic before you attend, giving rough details of the injury, it will help the vet to prepare for detailed emergency treatment.

A broken leg bone is very distressing for dog and owner. Nature, however, is very practical. Immediately after such injuries, the shock produces its own pain deadeners. Most dogs can also move adequately on three legs for a while, so it is not always necessary to attempt to carry the dog to the car. Do remember that a dog in shock may attempt to bite you if you interfere too much with the wound. For just such emergencies, as well as my dogs' general comfort, I always carry in the car a well-filled beanbag, covered by an artificial fleece and a blanket. This not only gives them well-earned rest after exercise or a hard day's work, but enables them to keep warm, dry and comfortable if injured. Most broken bones can be effectively repaired by modern orthopaedic surgery, so do not despair if such injuries occur.

THE WORKING DOG

Injuries

If a dog is acclimatised to most of the hazards it will meet in the field, it is amazing how few injuries it suffers. Most dogs thrust through dense cover at alarming speeds when stimulated by game, without coming to any great harm. Barbed-wire and fences are painful obstacles. As with all hazards the dog should be educated in its training to get through, under or over these. Once it has been pricked a time or two it learns a remarkable ability to judge the size of gap, the height of fence and the distance between barbed-wire strands and to balance this against the shape of its body and its jumping ability. This way it mostly stays clear of trouble.

On rare occasions dogs become impaled or 'hung' on barbed wire. It has happened to my dogs on several occasions. If they struggle they will be badly torn or may even break a leg. They are usually hanging upside down. I bawl 'stay' at them in my harshest tones, put an arm under the neck to take all the weight, and try to ease the belly, back legs and skin from the obstruction. It has always worked to date. Beware under these circumstances – your dog will understandably be in a state of panic and may well try to bite anything and anybody, including you, if you interfere precipitously. My dogs are well dominated from an early age and so far they have listened to me and become relaxed enough not to bite. If you cannot manage without injury to yourself, take off your jacket or top garment and cover the dog's head immediately before trying to intervene. HPRs make their intentions of biting very clear under these circumstances so prepare yourself mentally for such emergencies before they arise. You have been warned!

Dog fights

Dog fights are not uncommon among HPRs and it is relevant to consider them in this chapter. Some of these breeds can be considered as positively aggressive if allowed to be. I make this last point as it is important to prevent fights and anticipate at all times situations which can provoke fights, such as bones, possessiveness over handler, and dummies and birds not in use or in a heap. The main cause, however, is lack of positive dominance by the owner or handler. 'Pack law' basically dictates that it is the pack leader only that initiates a fight – this, of course, should be the handler/owner from an early age.

If a fight occurs with a dog on a lead it can usually be controlled or contained. If both are off the lead try training authority such as 'leave!' You can also try running away and calling your animal – it may work in the early stages when dogs are 'squaring up' to each other. Do not under any circumstances, interfere with hands to pull them apart: they will almost certainly bite you severely. The simplest remedy is to throw your jacket, waterproof or anything similar over to temporarily 'blind' them. I never recommend unnecessary physical violence but under these extreme circumstances the instep of the foot planted firmly into the ribs of each dog temporarily knocks the wind out of them and reduces them to a controllable state.

The damage dogs (or bitches) of this type do to each other is extensive and rapid to skin, muscle and bones – particularly of the neck and forelegs. Apply routine antiseptic treatment as described before. Deep bite wounds are always followed by septic infection, which gives the animal considerable misery and discomfort. All fights of a serious nature should therefore be followed by a visit to the vet for advice and treatment. Try to ensure that a visit to hospital for *you* is not necessary. Prevention is definitely better than cure in all aspects of dog fights!

Feeding for work

If you work your dog in the field for beating or picking up you must realise that the energy output of an HPR is very high. They therefore require up to four times their normal input of food on a working day if they are to maintain peak fitness, strength and bodily condition. Being primitive dogs, they may help themselves if they are hungry. Many years ago I saw one of my top working Weimaraner bitches eating a pheasant at midday on a hard pick up! She promptly returned to cover and delivered a further 13 pheasants without a mark on them. I now work all my dogs on a full meal before they go out in the morning, followed by a further large meal in the evening after working and resting on their return. Be warned – HPRs will not tolerate hunger pangs when 'food' is available. I do not find that this feeding is so essential with the majority of other working breeds.

Dehydration and exhaustion

HPRs are a tough group of dogs. Many of them will work until they drop, whether in training or on game. After a delivery of a difficult dummy or birds, they will sometimes lie down and pant with exhaustion and heat build-up in the body. They may even be dehydrated. It is important to have water near to hand. Cattle troughs are a marvellous cooling agent and thirst quencher. Apart from the water I carry, all my dogs are trained when young to search out water troughs and lie in them. They really take to them. Rivers, streams and ponds are not always at hand! An HPR rapidly learns to make the best use of available facilities. A short rest after a dip soon puts it into working trim again.

If your dog seems to have collapsed, put it in the shade, give water by mouth and wet the head and neck. Allow wind and air to circulate. Temporary recovery usually follows until more substantial water can be found.

BREEDING (or how to survive a whelping)

Before you decide that you are going to breed from your dog or bitch, take a long hard look at the pros and cons, especially when dealing with HPRs. 'It would be nice to have another pup from him/her' is not an objective reason, but an emotional one. Ask yourself the following questions. Have you shown the animal to prove that it conforms to roughly what the breed standard requires? Is its conformation sound? What about its temperament? Can you control it? Does it bite? Does it bark? Has it got natural working ability? Have you had it cleared of hereditary faults such as retinal atrophy, entropion, hip dysplasia or, indeed, poor temperament?

Assuming you find positive answers to these questions, consider whether it would be worth buying another pup, letting someone else have the problems of breeding, and whether it is worth while having your animal neutered – dog or bitch. Much has been written and continues to be written about the merits and demerits of neutering, both in and out of the veterinary profession. I have kept and worked many neutered dogs and spayed bitches. It makes not the slightest difference to their working ability or brainpower. They do not go stupid. There is a 10 per cent tendency to put on weight, which can easily be controlled by dietary input – in other words feeding according to the condition of the individual animal. There are sometimes changes in the coat colour and length, especially the red colours, following neutering. This is an inconvenience which can be controlled to a large degree by a razor comb.

Some bitches of HPR breeds live on a shorter fuse after a season in their 'false pregnancy' phase. Neutering them prevents these unwanted side effects and also prevents the possibility of womb trouble and resultant surgical correction in later life. It is also convenient – no twice-yearly seasons and therefore no restrictions on the bitches' exercise and work.

Dogs can be castrated by a simple operation of one day's duration. It stops them 'cocking their legs' every time there has been another dog or bitch in the area. Such territorial marking can be one of the preludes to fighting. Castration removes the male secondary sex characteristics and allows the dog to concentrate on his work or training rather than being occupied with other dogs or bitches whose scents are in the area.

For those of you who think these ideas are prejudiced, the Guide Dogs for the Blind Association, whose dogs work all the time, recommend castration or spaying at ten months of age just before maturity. It allows them to be just working dogs and companions without being distracted by hormonal influences and fluctuations.

The decision about neutering or breeding is yours. Do try to be objective and think of the future wellbeing of the breed in the field and as companion dogs as well as of your own personal interests.

Mating

Assuming that you decide to breed from your bitch after taking due note of the preceding precautions, the best age for producing a first litter is between two and five years. Most bitches come into season twice annually so you can arrange a litter to suit your own domestic arrangements. It is a good idea to have a vaginal swab taken on the first or second day of season. This will indicate any infection that may be present and this can be dealt with by a simple douche or 'washout'. Such vaginal infections are often responsible for infectious infertility.

Each season lasts for approximately 21 days. It starts with enormous enlargement of the vulva over 12–24 hours and the production of vaginal haemorrhage, which the bitch usually cleans up by licking. After roughly seven days, more mucous and less blood is produced. It is between the seventh and twentieth day that the bitch will be most likely to conceive. When ovulating and ready for mating she will swish the tail to one side when scratched at the base of the tail in the pelvic area. Each bitch varies slightly and mostly the bitch knows best – or the dog!

Select your stud dog with as much thought and care as you have given to your bitch. The same guiding principles apply concerning temperament, hereditary faults and so on. When introduced to the stud dog there is a preliminary sniffing and licking routine, accompanied by great excitement and 'play-capers' from both parties. This is usually followed by acceptance of the male by the bitch. Mating takes place, followed by roughly 20 minutes of the dog and bitch being 'tied'. During this period the dog goes through a contortion act after ejaculation and they stand back to back. A novice bitch may have to be restrained at this stage to prevent obvious possible damage to either party. Mating can be repeated after 48–72 hours when the same routine is followed. Sperm does last for 48 hours at least inside the bitch so more frequent matings are unnecessary.

Pregnancy

Pregnancy lasts for 63 days from the time of mating. Up to six days early or four days late should not be considered as abnormal. Pregnancy can be checked manually in the HPR at 3½–4 weeks of gestation. To date all blood tests are unreliable in the bitch and do not differentiate between a normal pregnancy and a false one. Pregnancy tests should be carried out by a veterinary surgeon to avoid harm and inaccuracies.

Worming should be carried out at least once against the roundworm *Toxocara canis*. This is probably best done during the last third of gestation. It removes adult roundworms from the bitch but does not affect the potential worm burden of the pups (see the section on parasites earlier).

Feeding should not be altered during the first six weeks of gestation. During the last three weeks, the normal routine protein intake should be approximately doubled. It is useful to add a good quality vitamin and mineral supplement during this period. It is much easier for a bitch to whelp in a fit condition. Excess feeding causes excess fat, weakens muscles and therefore adversely affects the bitch's general fitness. Food can be supplied ad lib once the bitch has whelped and lactation has commenced. This is the time of greatest demand on her resources. All bitches of the larger, more primitive breeds will supply adequate nutrition to their pups in the uterus even if they have to deplete their own muscles and reserves because of a poor diet.

Exercise should be maintained as usual during pregnancy. Swimming does no harm to bitch or pups. Some working bitches become indifferent to strenuous exercise and should go at their own pace. Other HPRs will work with enthusiasm to within a week of gestation without harm. Allow for each individual bitch's requirements. Take heart – abortion among large, healthy HPRs is a great rarity!

Whelping area

If you intend your bitch to whelp in an outdoor kennel with run complex where she usually lives, make sure that the whole area is clean and disinfected. The indoor area should be warm and well insulated. Temperatures of 70–80°F should be maintained consistently, without nightly drops during cold weather. The bitch should be comfortable and acclimatised to this environment at least seven days before she is due. Newspaper is popular as a box lining for the bitch to tear up and scatter, but I prefer hay (or wheat straw) which provides wonderful insulation and comfort and can be readily changed. Bitches seem to revel in making a 'nest' in hay.

If you make a whelping box elsewhere in a building or your home, use wood or chipboad. The box should be strongly constructed with a hinged lid for viewing. The height of the box should be such that the bitch is able to stand comfortably, and the length approximately 40 cm longer than the overall length of the bitch lying down. The width of the box, in turn, should be 40 cm more than the overall bitch's width. The width and length measurements allow for a 'guard rail' of approximately 6 cm to be erected round the inner circumference. This enables the bitch to lie down without crushing the pups in the early days after whelping. Lid and sides should all be insulated on the outside to preserve heat and prevent the bitch and pups demolishing the insulation! A 'pop hole' should be cut in the front at the bottom left or right to allow the bitch access and egress at will. This should be covered with a piece of material to prevent draughts.

By these means you can create the 'den' effect of the primitive dog. The bitch also produces enough heat from her own body to maintain a comfortable temperature for herself and her pups. The pups, who have no means of heat regulation for the first five days after birth, are then able to suckle, sleep and relax.

Much has been made of the infra-red lamp as a source of heat. This is cumbersome and quite unnecessary if the preceding recommendations are followed. Some eminent authorities have stated that the lamp, by causing a cold draught in an exposed situation, is responsible for chilling pups and therefore causing early deaths. The argument goes that the lamp warms the pup's surface, the hot air caused above the skin rises, and this draws in cold air down the sides and chills the pup. It is easier, simpler and more effective to insulate the area and let the bitch get on with her natural protective work. The 'den' effect also gives a great sense of security to the bitch – very important in preventing stress.

Whelping

Bitches normally show a vague uneasiness approximately 48 hours before whelping. They tear up the bedding material and may refuse food, although most HPR bitches will eat some food. They may drink more and need frequent intervals of being let outside to urinate or just wander round. Observe all this with equanimity if you are able to do so. A disturbed owner tends to lead to a disturbed bitch.

Imminent parturition is indicated by obvious straining by the bitch. The intervals are firstly every hour or so, becoming shorter until quite strong contractions occur every two minutes. These two-minute-interval strainings can go on for two hours before you need to be worried. If you are worried consult your veterinary surgeon. Most whelpings are during the night and you will receive a more relaxed reception to your call if you have warned him or her of the expected whelping date well in advance.

After or during this period of straining a pup should appear. It may pop completely out of the vagina – so much the better. The bitch may groan at the time of these final expulsive forces. If the pup is covered in a membrane or afterbirth, the bitch usually licks and chews it off immediately. The pup breathes. It tries and often succeeds in finding a teat and suckling straightaway.

If the head is presented from the vulva you can assist if you think the pup is stuck by putting some tissues over it – it is very slippery – then pulling and rotating at the same time. This causes further straining with hopefully the same result – a live pup. Membranes can and should also be removed with tissues if the bitch does not oblige. *Do not* interfere at all unless you have to. Most bitches are very sensible and do the right things themselves in the right order.

The remainder of the pups are born in a similar manner. The intervals between the birth of each pup should not exceed two hours. If the bitch is relaxed all is usually well. Take the bitch outside for a walk round and for urination etc. It makes her feel more comfortable and assists in the presentation of the next pup. If it is the middle of the night take a torch with you – she may pass a pup outside. If she does, rub it down with a warm towel and replace in the whelping box.

A warm, sweet drink of tea or milk assists the energy of both bitch and midwife! Some bitches enjoy a meal in the middle of whelping but most do not. Once again cater for individual variations in different bitches.

If the bitch appears to be clumsy you can remove pups to a heated enclosed box. A cardboard box containing hot-water bottles and towels is adequate, but ensure that the pups suckle at intervals of not less than one hour. The suckling obviously nourishes the pups; at the same time the stimulating effect on the bitches' teats encourages milk letdown and further contractions, enabling the whole process of whelping to proceed.

Maintain a quiet, relaxed atmosphere at all times during the whelping and do not disturb the bitch more than necessary. Hopefully you will now finish with a relaxed bitch surrounded by contented puppies, all in a warm environment.

Most bitches do not require medication before, during or after whelping in normal circumstances. For the fidgety, anxious type, I use a homeopathic remedy of Pulsatilla 30 given at two-hour intervals immediately prior to and during whelping. This seems to calm the bitch and smooth the normal process of whelping for her. These tablets are available from homoeopathic chemists and some health stores.

If your bitch is unable to whelp for whatever reason the pups (or some of them) can be born by Caesarean section. This operation does not usually interfere with the normal rearing sequences of the pups. You must be guided here by your veterinary surgeon, but do not be in a hurry for this operation. HPRs are strong dogs and can usually deliver their own pups given enough time.

Having finished whelping the bitch lies comfortably with a litter of pups varying in number from four to twelve. They should all be trying to suckle. You should take her for a short walk outside to stretch herself and urinate etc. If she is dirty and green behind you can shampoo the rear end to cleanse it. I always use a few drops of proprietary hypochlorite in the water as an antiseptic. Encourage her milk flow with a warm, sweet drink. If she wants to eat let her have her normal food. She will be anxious to return to her pups and be with them, so let her do so and leave them to feed in peace. By dawn she will have cleaned up the pups and eaten most of the afterbirth during the whelping. This is all quite normal. She will almost certainly have copious green-coloured diarrhoea for two days after whelping – this is also normal and will resolve itself. The umbilical cords on the pups dry up rapidly with no attention and drop off within 48 hours. Milk letdown occurs during the 48 hours following whelping and is stimulated by the suckling of the puppies. This applies throughout their rearing – there is very often no apparent milk in the mammary glands, but it is immediately available when stimulation occurs from the pups.

Food for the bitch is not important during the first 48-hours post-partum but fluids are. Once she starts to feed, remember she is working very hard at the milk production. I recommend feeding with the normal quantity and type of food but increasing the frequency to three times daily. The amounts bitches consume can easily be up to 6 lbs of protein daily, but it will all be utilised to maintain the bitch herself and her milk flow. I do not recommend special foods or baby foods. Your bitch is perfectly able to manufacture milk from a water and protein intake. Too much variation from her normal food will tend to cause diarrhoea with resultant disturbance in the milk flow. It is also important not to have her and her pups disturbed by strangers examining the litter for at least two weeks. Infection may be intro-duced as well as stress caused to the bitch.

Tail docking and removal of dewclaws

This is a controversial topic. Dewclaw removal is certainly essential for working breeds. A great deal has been said, on the other hand, about the demerits of tail docking. Most of the points put forward seem to me to be emotionally overloaded and lacking in objective thought. The subject requires full debate by those involved, including those members of the veterinary profession who have experience of the working problems involved.

It is certainly unnecessary to dock breeds for the show ring. However, let the Kennel Club and breed societies sort out the problem on an international basis so that we can have uniformity of thought and positive direction from our governing bodies. They must not shirk their responsibilities to promote debates and discussions at this level.

For working dogs and large dogs the considerations are different. Many years ago, when they hunted deer or wild boar in triples, they damaged their tails and bled severely. As guard dogs the tails could be grasped to restrain them. In modern circumstances any breed consis-tently going through heavy cover (brambles, etc.) will at some stage strip the tail end, which bleeds profusely and becomes chronic in spite of any and all remedial treatment. Large dogs in confined spaces also tend to bang their tail tips on kennels, doorways and furniture with the same consequences. Surgical docking at this stage is drastic, painful for at least ten days and requires considerable surgical skills. As for cruelty and mutilation, these are emotive words.

Docking and removal of dewclaws is carried out two or three days after birth. It is bloodless, almost painless, rapid (about 30 seconds) and without subsequent problems if performed in a skilled manner. I have demonstrated this many times. The pups return to the nest, they do not whimper and they suckle immediately the bitch is reintroduced. I consider it no more 'cruel and mutilating' than circumcision to the human baby, which is rapidly forgotten by the recipient!

Puppy development

Your pups should now grow and develop normally. If they show signs of dullness or become thin-belllied, seek professional advice immediately.

At three weeks old the pups are almost on their feet. They are inquisitive and start to explore their surroundings. They will play and play-fight among themselves. The puppies should all be wormed at this age. Piperazine tablets are effective and should be given first at three weeks old, with further doses at four, five and seven weeks. This controls the worst of the worm burden (see the section on parasites). Worms are passed within 24 hours and cleaned up by the bitch, so worm her on each occasion 24 hours after the pups have had their treatment.

At three weeks the puppies also start to eat food as well as taking the bitch's milk. They should be introduced to high-protein animal foods as soon as possible (see the section in this chapter on feeding). Mine are fed three or four times a day on fish, scrap meat, finely minced raw green tripe and mashed hard-boiled eggs. This is mixed with wholemeal biscuit meal in roughly equal proportions by volume. Water is added to make it into a softer consistency. For the first meal or two they may have to be finger-fed. This rapidly becomes unnecessary; they soon feed with enthusiasm. Bones should also be introduced into the nest area and the puppies will learn to lick and chew them. Make sure several are available or they will become very possessive over them.

At this age they should all be handled sensibly at least twice daily – preferably more. This, as we have said, is the important human imprint age which is so necessary in the prevention of nervousness. The pups start using an outdoor run from this time on and soon learn to defecate outside the bedding area. It is useful to walk round the garden area with the 'pack' as their education in the outside environment continues to develop. They also begin listening to the 'calling' noises of the human voice.

As the pups grow it is advisable to feed them from individual feeding bowls or at least from several bowls. This tends to prevent aggressive action at feeding times. Additional milk is not necessary but can be given in small quantities. The more you feed the pups the less they will take from the bitch. She will start to build herself up again so that she can go back to normal living and work soon after the pups go to their new homes at eight weeks. And by following the advice outlined here you will have made sure that the new owners obtain the sort of well-conditioned pup that you would want to buy yourself.

12

ALTERNATIVE USES

Diana Durman-Walters

FALCONRY

Today, the modern falconer's dog is exemplified in the HPR. No longer is there the need for a kennel of dogs with single talents; instead one has the choice of a type of dog which can tackle a variety of tasks with method and considerable accomplishment.

The newcomer to falconry will inevitably ask at what stage of the game he or she should think about dog ownership and which dog and type to choose from a litter. Without the slightest shadow of doubt the dog must come into the house before the hawk and the animal's training must take place without the added pressure of trying to train a hawk at the same time. If both hawk and dog are novices in the field then the likelihood of achieving a satisfactory standard from both at the same time is remote, if only because both are likely to do something desperately wrong at the same time. Whilst this may conjure up an amusing scenario, we are trying to achieve harmony between man, hawk and dog. The common link between all three is training.

Preliminary training

One of the breeds of HPR which has recently made a name for itself in falconry is the German wire-haired pointer. Rugged, versatile, intelligent and a keen hunter, this breed has all the elements of a very trainable dog. Having chosen a friendly but composed puppy and made it familiar with sit, stay and recall over its first twelve months of informal training, you are then ready to begin serious training. The training programme should be consistent, approximately 20 to 30 minutes each day in the initial stages. These periods can be broken into two 10–15-minute sessions, one in the morning and one in the afternoon if an entire period is not possible.

One of the first things the youngster must learn is to walk on the right-hand side of the handler. The vast majority of falconers carry their hawks on their left hand, so the dog must walk on the opposite side in order not to upset the bird. The latter, in its turn, can keep its eye on the dog. Again, a pup that is calm and placid is not likely to upset a nervous hawk. Having established that it must walk on the right, do all your 'heel' work in this fashion. By now the dog should be capable of walking off the lead to the command of 'heel', keeping pace with you until you deem it time for it to run free. Periods of free play are essential when training, as the pup will begin to relate these sessions to training and start to find the sessions enjoyable.

You must make a conscious decision whether or not to bring retrieving as a skill into the training. Many people ask me whether this is desirable in a falconry dog for they have, I suspect, colourful visions of the dog bringing back the hawk from its kill. Not so. These dogs were bred to their task and one correctly trained will not see the hawk on its kill in the middle of a field as a potential retrieve but will view it objectively; the hawk has taken legitimate quarry which is outside the remit of the dog. Naturally, we do not leave the dog to make this decision but it will become part of its education.

It is important to select a small field to work in as large unfenced areas mean that the pup has the means to run out of earshot and out of control. A general misconception is that once a dog has run off into the distance there is little you can do about it other than challenge it on its return and hit it to show the error of its ways. The only result is that it understands not that it is wrong to run away, but that it is painful to return. When a dog has careered off into the sunset, having apparently been struck stone deaf, you must at once follow after it to correct its mistake. The very fact that you are running after it, uttering ancient Cymric in its direction, is usually enough to stop the animal in its tracks; it will then return to you or run around you, aware that all is not well. Take hold of the dog, replace the lead, smartly walk it back to the spot where it disobeyed you and begin again. Dogs hate to think they are getting it wrong because this places them in an invidious position in the pack. The fact that the pack is just you and the dog makes no difference – it will still equate your action to pack discipline. And that is the way it should be: you give the orders and the dog obeys.

One obvious reason why a dog will take off is a hare or rabbit – it is hell bent on showing you several reasons why you have no need to buy a lurcher! Coursing is best left to the experts and should be avoided like the plague with your young impressionable puppy. It makes sense therefore to train the youngster in areas devoid of game.

Now you can introduce the whistle for all your commands. Dogs have the infuriating habit of being unable to understand perfect English! For instance, take the case of rabbit chasing. In order for the dog to have got so close to a rabbit it will probably have been locating the scent unbeknown to you, tipped the rabbit from its seat and set off. Shouting for the animal to return is useless.

Consider the case of Roger. This is the name of a dog, not the handler. Roger's job was to locate rabbits out in the field for a goshawk, point them and allow the hawk the opportunity to slip at them. The only problem was that the dog did not understand. On the first encounter his handler had been quite effectively quartering him across rough pasture when he spun into a riveting point. The handler sensed that something was about to happen and talked animatedly to the dog, cautioning it against any subversive action. At that moment the rabbit bolted from its seat and sped towards a distant copse. And so did Roger! The handler began to scream the dog's name as loudly as possible – an action which Roger interpreted as an encouraging cheer, nicking into fifth gear and disappearing in hot pursuit of the rabbit. Meanwhile the hawk, seeing the fleeing rabbit, had also taken off. Now man, hawk and dog were all converging on the copse. The hawk, noting the futility of the chase, landed in the tallest tree she could find and remained there. Roger had vanished, eventually to return looking pleased with himself.

Moral: don't call a dog Roger; in fact don't call it at all but use a whistle. Dogs that point become mesmerised by the quarry before them. Their natural instincts as hunters come to the fore and it becomes difficult for them to distinguish between what you would like them to do and their desire to hunt and kill to satisfy their compulsive reflex action. The animal's name does not convey a command, whereas a whistle blown to the order 'sit' will rap out an instant command which is far more effective.

The three commands that must be taught are sit, turn right/left and recall. Normally, these are given as one long blast, two blasts and staccato pips respectively. At the moment a rabbit or pheasant leaves the covert the handler, who should be right up with the pointing dog, must have the whistle ready in his mouth to give the stop command – sit there until told otherwise! Surprisingly, once you have done this half a dozen times it will become patently obvious to the dog that it must have nothing further to do with events. The whistle must now be your only point of contact with the dog.

One of the most important aspects of training is to keep the dog's attention 100 per cent of the time. Eye-to-eye contact is vital. A dog that will look you in the face when you are about to give a command is at one with you. Such a dog will hang on your every word and will become a pleasure to work with. The problem with training a dog for falconry is not that it is going to perform its tasks in a manner alien to a shot-over dog, but that it will have to perform them for a hawk or falcon and be relied upon to play its part while the falconer concentrates on his bird. He must rely totally on the dog and be confident it will not run amok. As most dogs will not be required to retrieve whilst hawking their skills must be concentrated solely on pointing and steadiness.

The majority of falconers' dogs will be used in conjunction with hawks, hence their work will be confined to low-ground pastures interspersed with woodland, and rabbits will be the principal quarry. It is vital then that the dog is steady to fur. A minority of falconers will want their dogs to concentrate exclusively on upland gamebirds, such as red grouse and black cock. These dogs will be run in the traditional manner, quartering for a point, locating the quarry and flushing it. The attractive feature of the HPR is that it can hunt both upland ground and low ground, something pointers and setters have not been bred to do.

Dogs for hawks

The dog needs to be a jack of all trades and its training will have to take into account that it will meet most types of game and distractions. Its training will, of necessity, be longer than that of the dog used exclusively on the moor. It must be able to point partridges, pheasants, rabbits and hares, and also be capable of dealing with woodcock, snipe, squirrels and moorhens for certain hawks. At once it becomes obvious why the dog must be trained long before the untrained hawk is acquired.

As rabbits are the staple quarry of most austringers (hawk owners) we will deal with this aspect of training first. Many austringers use ferrets with their hawks in conjunction with the dog. This combination works well if there are two of you to control the hunters! The dog may have been used to indicate that a warren is being used and once the ferret is down the hole will be expected to lie quietly beside the handler, on no account giving chase if a rabbit has been bolted. This is practice in the most practical sense.

The young dog will be taken out ferreting without the hawk, and whilst being held on a strong lead will firmly be told 'no' every time a rabbit appears. A check chain with lead is very effective as this enhances the command and forces the dog to do as you require.

Tell the dog to lie down at the warren before you put the ferret

Ghyllbeck Grif, a Münster owned by Mr G. Hargreaves

FT Ch. Riscoris Fleur de Lys, a Brittany owned by Mrs A. Lewis

Sh. Ch. Castlefield Rhapsody in Blue and Russetmantle Jan,
vizslas owned by Mrs A. Coombe

*Freshiska of Hawksmoor (GWP) and Ellie the Harris Hawk,
owned by Mr J. Powell*

down. In this position it will be more difficult for it to make a move in the direction of the rabbit as the dog will first have to get on its feet, giving you a chance to correct it. You will give the dog a verbal command in this situation as you can enforce it without the dog running off. Once you are confident it is beginning to understand the rules of the game then you can begin to allow it to remain at a warren without its lead, giving the lie down command on the whistle; at a later date you can replace this with a quiet whistle or hiss through your teeth.

This particular aspect of training may take a dozen outings and even months to get right, but do not give up until the dog knows exactly what is required of it. It is easy to do the job by half measures, with the misguided notion that the dog will pick it up as time goes on. As mentioned before, dogs have a great knack of failing to understand the spoken word and steadiness can be acquired only through repetition. However, just because the dog at home will sit perfectly at holes in which it has indicated rabbits does not mean it looks on rabbits lying out in pasture as the same thing. Once a dog is free ranging, whether it will listen to you and co-operate is all a question of training.

Let us look again at the youngster still in training in fields without game and see where we go from here. In order that the dog can seek ground game it must be allowed to run and quarter. Some dogs quarter naturally, whilst others have to be instructed so that, by being given a pattern, they can systematically sweep across a field searching for ground scent. Quartering is method hunting. It allows precision and avoids random searching which could flush unwanted game and spoil the chances of a suitable slip for the hawk.

To set your pup in motion sit it at your side with the wind in its face. Stand a few feet back from the dog with your arm fully outstretched, indicate the direction in which it must begin and cast it off with the words 'get on'. Standing back from the dog allows it to keep an eye on you for visual direction, at the same time looking in front to see where to go. If there is a hedge, tree or wall to the side so much the better as the dog will naturally run to these objects out of curiosity. Once it has reached the barrier or object, give two pips on the whistle to turn it to come across in front of you in the opposite direction. As you begin to walk in the direction you want your dog to move, it will automatically follow. Now it is learning the rudiments of quartering. At all times in these formative lessons hand signals must be given. A youngster hearing a command does not necessarily understand what it means, so until competent always give a visual signal as well.

Once mastered by both dog and handler it is time to have a look at the youngster in action. Already the dog has been taught how to control itself near the warren, it understands the word 'no' and, most important of all, knows the meaning of the stop whistle. This last is vital before it enters a gamey area.

Having cast the dog out into the field for the first time you may find that the hitherto normally obedient pup is now wandering aimlessly over the ground and failing to create a pattern to its work. This is because the ground is soaked with the scent of animals and birds, all of which it would like to investigate at once. Stop the dog with the stop whistle and when it looks at you recall it. At this point it will probably realise that it is not doing it correctly but will not know why. Sit the dog down as if you were about to begin a lesson on quartering at home and keep it very much on a tight pattern over a small area.

Many people say to me that HPRs will not range, i.e. they will not get out a long distance to hunt. This is a popular myth and it is far more difficult to keep a dog in a confined space than to let it have its head and career off to cover enormous tracts of land. Dogs of all these breeds from good hunting stock have a natural tendency to want to work wide of the handler. With their drive and natural good noses they cut swathes through the field as they push ever onward for a point. They must be taught at an early age that their ground work is a pattern of 30 metres either side of the handler and no more than 20 metres in front. In a wood this should be even closer. Once a dog has successfully completed its first hawking season then it will be possible to allow it to work a little wider – provided the dog is always within sight.

Often, when walking up to a warren, you will find rabbits lying out in a field. These make excellent slips for the hawk and are far more exciting than bolted rabbits. But to locate rabbits in this fashion you must have a good pointer. From a practical point of view this can be any of the HPR breeds but the German wire-haired pointer fits the bill to perfection as its tough, dense coat copes very well with brambles and dense cover.

Pointing is a phenomenon that occurs in most dogs and in the specialised pointing breeds has been honed to a fine degree. Any dog locating a rabbit or bird will stop for a second and look at it before trying to snatch at it. I have watched many Labradors and spaniels give a very good account of themselves pointing. What makes pointers different is that their mission in life is to find game and remain rigid in the area, clearly indicating to all concerned that they have found game. On many occasions I have watched one of our dogs remain on point for 15 minutes, due entirely to a wayward falcon failing to come into position over the dog.

Because we are hawking we clearly do not want the dog to retrieve any quarry; this is the hawk's job. But how do you get that over to a young dog? This is the most difficult task as it will be tempted to 'peg' the bird or rabbit in front and then will pick it up and hand it to you.

Pointers can do this with lightning efficiency. How can you stop it?

Imagine we are again in the rabbit field. The young dog is making a presentable job of quartering the field when suddenly it spins round and locks on to point. You put your whistle in your mouth and walk quietly but quickly to the dog, taking a path such that it can see you from the corner of its eye. This will avoid the dog rushing in to snatch the quarry in a fit of jealousy, thinking you are going to deprive it of the rabbit. Speak quietly and confidently, saying 'steady' or 'stay', and gently slip the lead over the dog's neck. Then tell it to 'get in'. The dog may for a moment refuse but your urgency says 'I must chase'. It will jump in, either feet first to push the game up, or mouth first to retrieve it. Whichever, you immediately tell the dog 'no' by blasting the 'sit' command on the whistle and jerking it up tight on the lead. No one will be more surprised than the dog, which will stare long and hard after the fleeing rabbit. Do not let the dog off the lead otherwise it will be off in hot pursuit of the vanishing prize. Then take the dog to a different part of the field to work. If it tries to return to the area where it found the rabbit scold it with the words 'no, leave' and insist that the dog quarters where you wish it to.

We now approach the time when your youngster needs to be introduced to the hawks. Plan to take it out with a friend who has a well-made hawk and ask him or her to call the hawk to the lure, which will then be dragged in front of the dog with the hawk eating from it. Try to make the dog familiar with routines. However, do not allow the dog to be a nuisance to someone else's hawk as nothing annoys a falconer more than a dog upsetting his hawk so that, perhaps, it takes off into the next county or takes stand in a tree for three hours.

A dog will make its most serious errors with hawks when it discovers they fly. Objects moving away from a dog will always incite a chase so it has to learn that the hawk is definitely not to be pursued or caught and that on no account is there to be a contest over who should have the rabbit. The dog must learn that once it has pointed the rabbit that is the end of its task.

Harris hawks and red-tailed hawks are normally placid enough to allow a dog in the field with them while they are eating, so get the youngster to lie down on the lead. Place the lure about 30 feet in front of him and call the hawk to it. As the bird begins to eat so the dog can savour the moment. Do this as often as possible until the dog becomes quite blasé.

Dogs have a great curiosity where hawks are concerned, particularly in what they have caught. Because they have pointed it for the hawk they like to know the outcome and are often tempted to see at close range what the bird is clutching. One of my German wire-haired pointers got her kicks in this fashion. She had an addiction to danger that nearly always ended with her screaming the place down.

On one occasion she had just produced an excellent point on a pheasant which, on being flushed, took off at a rate of knots towards a wood. The goshawk, keyed up for the flush, sprang from the glove in hot pursuit, gaining ground all the time. Quilt and I set off in the direction of the hawk and the wood.

All was silent. Normally the gos would call to me but the silence indicated that she had caught her bird. Being a clever little dog Quilt busied herself backwards and forwards through the wood looking for the hawk (she could probably hear the faintest rustle of bells, inaudible to my ears). She could not resist going in to see what the gos had caught. Crawling on her belly, she eased her way under the dense brambles as if to take in the pheasant aroma once again. The gos eyed her balefully, raising her crest and extending her wings into an exaggerated mantle. Swivelling her eyes better to observe this canine idiot, she let fly with both feet, sinking her claws firmly into the now departing rear end of the dog. Quilt emerged like a wailing banshee with the furious goshawk still attached. However, the bird, realising it was courting disaster because of the foliage, let go and returned to her kill, leaving a much chastened wire-hair.

It pays to let young dogs know that hawks can hurt and once learnt this lesson is usually never forgotten, though there will be exceptions to this rule. Whenever possible take the young dog out with hawks other than your own at first so that you can concentrate on the dog. If you can work your youngster for a season before you get your hawk so much the better.

Dogs for falcons

Dogs used in this branch of the sport are no longer specialists in only one discipline. Falcons flown on upland gamebirds require a pointer whose sole task is to locate birds. But today's falconer is nearly always also an austringer so he will need a dog capable of working lowlands as well. This is where the HPR fits the bill perfectly.

For the past ten years we have almost exclusively used German wire-haired pointers for moorland work. Although a medium-paced pointer, it has great powers of endurance. The wire-hair's typical deep chest provides lung room to haul it up tiring contours and yet help propel it over flat ground at a seemingly never-ending pace. Puppies that come from strong bird-finding lines, particularly from Bavaria and Austria, will be the dogs best capable of performing exclusive bird work. In order to achieve this, the pup must be kept away from rabbits and their ground scent in training. Dogs that need to locate birds require a much higher head carriage to locate the trailing, drifting scents left behind by gamebirds; rabbits succeed in teaching a pup to keep its head close to the ground, a habit it often has difficulty breaking. A dog holding its head low on a grouse moor will have problems coming to terms with scent as well as eventually running into its birds.

Training for falcons follows the same basic work used in training for hawks. The dog must be capable of sit, stay, lie down, turn right/ left and recall. All this is done by whistle and hand signals. The dog must also be very, very steady with the falcons. Its work will be some considerable distance from the handler with the falcon overhead waiting for its cue to begin the stoop and pursuit. From anything up to 100 metres away the dog must be capable of flushing on command from a shout given by the falconer. Once the falcon is committed the dog must sit to the flush and on no account charge in to the falcon to seize her quarry, or, worse still, knock her off the quarry, so making her unwilling to fly while that dog is in the area.

Young dogs being trained purely for the falcon will need to begin their training on the low ground where there are pheasants and partridges. The more delicate, more subtle scents of these birds make detection harder, thus teaching dogs infinitely more than would the very strong scent of grouse. Strangely enough, dogs that have only learned their skills on grouse are left ill-equipped to cope with the refined scents of low-ground game.

Because scent is the all-important factor for the pointer, it must learn that cover such as bushes, trees and tussocks of grass all help to divert direct scent, thus confusing the dog's idea of the bird's location. With a high head carriage the dog must learn to use its nose like a beautifully refined Hoover to interpret accurately the disseminated scent. The dog instinctively knows what it is looking for and will lock on to point on finding it. It will learn how to run round the wind when it is not blowing to advantage and will begin to build up a mental picture of likely areas that may hold potential quarry and investigate these before all else. But only on low ground will a dog get the diversity of terrain that will give it the education it needs.

Bearing all this in mind it will be obvious that to obtain a good bird dog will require plenty of practice in the field. Young dogs of 18 months of age are suitable for their first season's work, provided they are not expected to work for hours on end at their task. Ideally, it is best to work the youngster with an older, experienced dog. This removes the burden from the youngster's shoulders and will help eliminate mistakes.

When we are working a moor we have a team of three dogs, which means that each will run for about 15 minutes and will gain 30 minutes rest. This is invaluable, especially if the ground is very hard going. Keeping one dog in action all the time will eventually break its pace, so that you could do the job quicker yourself. As these dogs need to run vast distances they require the power and enthusiasm to do so.

On a moor there is usually little to distract a dog other than hares and sheep. Very often sheep are on the low ground in August and September and are no problem. Nevertheless it is vital to make sure your dog has been trained to know sheep. No farmer likes to see a dog coursing his prize blackface ewes until they are in a panic at the bottom of a glen. It is essential that the pup has been trained to be steady to fur. Remember that the ultimate goal is a dog on staunch point, with the falcon waiting overhead and a dead grouse at the end of the chase.

It is worth noting that over the years I have seen many HPRs in all their aspects and none has been more obedient than the falconer's dog. This is surely a credit to training and discipline and says much for the trainability of HPRs.

DEER-TRACKING

Of all the disciplines that a gundog will be taught, none is more exacting, or will take longer to achieve a desired result, than tracking deer and working with a stalker. It is not simply a case of following up a scent trail. It requires concentration, single-mindedness and plenty of practical work. Dogs embarking on this career will need to be around 18–24 months old to cope with the training.

Despite the fact that there are many stalkers in Britain and a large number of clients from overseas (particularly for roe deer), the development of the tracking dog has been virtually non-existent. On the Continent such a state of affairs is unheard of and all hunters, if not possessing their own dogs, have access to 'tracking stations' where they can call upon the services of a professional tracker to locate a wounded animal. The stalker pays for this service.

Small endurance dogs were used, which had been bred from bloodhound stock, and their noses are uniquely adapted to the role. These blood-tracking dogs have the ability to follow minute drops of blood which may have lain as an old trail for up to four days. They are persistent and remorseless in their quest and will not be deterred until the deer is found. However, as with all old breeds that are highly specialised, they have been overtaken by the versatile hunting dog – the HPR. Not that they do it any better – they could not – but these dogs were so useful in other forms of hunting that it made sense to teach them also to track deer. If you are keeping a dog solely for deer work it pays not to diversify it into other fields; all its energies can be mobilised for the task ahead and its mind left free to cope with the difficult tasks in store.

For two years running I spent time in Germany watching the training and trialling of these dogs on deer, as well as on all other aspects. Numerically, the biggest breed there is the German wire-haired pointer and all trials and field events are dominated by this versatile breed. The majority of people in Britain will not use their wire-hairs for tracking simply because this is not normally a part of their straightforward shooting duties, but for those who have acquired a wire-hair purely for stalking there is no better breed.

It is tempting to suppose that any gundog can be used for tracking. After all, springers and Labradors have good noses and are clever gundogs. Unfortunately, however, they lack the intense concentration required for the job. In Germany there is a flourishing interest in Labradors from this country. These dogs have to compete in trials if they are to be used for breeding. Part of the test is tracking, which they complete favourably, but when it comes to endurance tracking and the going gets tough the Labrador finds it difficult to compete with the utterly persistent HPRs, whose concentration never wavers.

One of the reasons why an HPR has to be more mature for this kind of training is that a great deal of the work will be out of sight of the handler, who therefore requires to know that the dog can be relied on to locate the deer and indicate in some manner that it has done so. It is possible to train the dog to work at all times within sight of the handler, but the woods have to be of the open, broad-leaved variety usually holding fallow and, to a lesser degree, roe.

As all training for deer-tracking is the same, let us look at the most difficult, yet most common terrain, a plantation forest. These dark, tightly grouped complexes offer little opportunity for the stalker to find a wounded deer, so he must have a dog to do the job for him. The stalker will have only a vague idea in which direction the deer has vanished, so he must rely on the dog to find its scent and follow it to its conclusion. This is not an easy task when you can give no assistance to the dog.

Once the dog has located the deer it must tell the stalker that it has found it. It may start howling and baying until you come, or bring you a thong tied to a collar round its neck. If the woods are open it will wear a special tracking collar and lead you to the deer. Obviously it will have to be trained for whichever of these methods you decide to use.

The most difficult of all is 'tortvebeller' or giving tongue. Very few dogs will actually do this and sustain the belling for up to 30 minutes! 'Bringsel', or bringing you the thong, is easier to teach, whilst the tracking collar is easiest of all three. We will return to these methods later. But whichever method is used the dog must shut from its mind any inclination to hunt or point whilst tracking and concentrate solely on the scent trail. In particular, it must ignore the active scent of any other deer that may have crossed the trail it is pursuing.

As with all training, results are achieved by giving rewards. You will need to have to hand ¼ litre deer's blood or, if you cannot obtain this, the same amount of bull's blood, to which has been added 1 teaspoon of salt. Stirred well this can be put in a suitable container and left in the freezer till required. You should also have lungs from a deer, dried then frozen, and a fresh deer skin, or better still a roe carcass. It is prudent to point out that the young dog should again have received basic training so that it understands the disciplines of sit, stay, heel, recall and lie down. With this you cannot even begin training in deer-tracking.

Now we are going to lay a trail for it that will test its nose and ability to follow a very simple scent. Take a stick (broom handles make very good accessories) and nail a piece of sponge about 2 inches square on the end. Dip the sponge into your blood container and leave a mark on the ground. Begin to lay a very simple trail, with two or three blood marks every 6 feet or so along a zig-zag line of 100 metres. At the end of the trail place the roe carcass or the skin. On top put a reward of a good piece of dried lung or a chunk of tripe. Walk well away from the trail, leave the scent to gather for 20 minutes and then fetch the dog. Put a stick or marker at the start of the trail otherwise you will find it difficult to recall exactly where it is.

Place a leather collar on the dog to which is attached a very long length of line. Lift up the dog's front leg and pass the line underneath to stop any undue pressure on its throat while it is trying to work. The moment the collar has been attached the dog will realise something different is about to happen. Take it to the starting point and make it sit down. With the command 'stay', go to the start of the trail and bend over as if examining it. The dog will be filled with curiosity. What are you looking at?

Go back to the dog and bring it to the start. Point to the ground where you were and the dog will at once realise there is blood there and will be keen to follow it. Take hold of the line and gently pay it out. The chances are the dog will imagine it knows how to find the 'runner' and will want to career off at 70 m.p.h. to find it. On no account let it. Steady the dog with the lead and the word 'steady' but resist the temptation to steer or guide it. As it gets near the end of the trail it will see the roe and probably run up to it. Encourage it to take its reward with much praise and patting. Do no more that day. This type of lesson needs to be done only twice a week at the most, but must be done correctly.

The next lesson is a slightly longer trail, only this time you are going to make sure the trail has been laid downwind, and someone else is going to lay the trail for you. Dogs soon learn to follow only your body scent, and if the trail is into the wind they can detect the deer without having to track it. Furthermore, as you will not know where the trail is, get your helper to mark the zig-zag with small sticks in the ground every metre. This will tell you whether the dog is following the trail exactly.

If the dog is slow grasping what is required then it is quite permissible in the early stages to leave rewards of small pieces of tripe or lung along the trail. Cover them with a dead leaf or grass so that the dog comes upon them rather than sees them. If it fails along the trail or wanders off it trying to wind-scent the deer *stop it immediately*. Do not scold but make it sit and then, picking it up in your arms, put it back on the exact spot where it became confused. Point to the ground and begin again.

Should the dog begin to make frequent mistakes leave the lesson alone and do not try again for a couple of days. All this work must be done on grass fields during the formative training. To make it hard by using the floor of a wood will defeat the object, and furthermore you may end up by losing your temper. You must stay cool at all times.

Provided that all goes well you can now begin to lay trails on the forest floor. Whether it is pine needles or leaf mould, it will now be more difficult for the dog to locate a blood track because of the composition of the ground and the fact that other animals may have crossed it or be lying in cover. Use less blood on the ground, so that instead of two or three blobs every 6 feet you leave only one. Also make the trails longer and allow a greater period to elapse before you start.

Whilst the dog is working the trail you may find that the deer-tracking lead is not practicable in the forest so you may decide to use the bringsel or tortvebeller. With the former the dog will wear on its collar a shortened lead with a thong attached, comprising a stick covered in leather. When the dog has found the deer at the end of the trail put the thong in its mouth and ask the dog to fetch it to you. Make a big fuss of it and slowly but surely on each occasion it will want to pick up the thong and give it to you. Now you can elect to have a short lead of about 6 inches with the thong attached which the dog will readily throw into its mouth on finding the deer. You can now begin to allow it to follow small tracks and when it comes back to you with the thong in its mouth tell it to return with you so that you can see where the deer lies. It takes a little time for the dog to grasp the fact that it must indicate the deer to you, but practice will eventually make perfect.

The tortvebeller really requires a dog which is a noisy barker, something that is actively discouraged in kennel and is often difficult to bring out in the animal. One method is to encourage the dog to bark for its 'dinner'; only when it does this will it be fed. Once it begins to bark then encourage it to continue for two or three minutes at a time. Always provide a reward at the end of a barking session. If you can get it to do this then accompany its food with a deer skin, and eventually show it the real thing to which, you hope, it will bark. You will now need to build up the dog's endurance at barking which will become a mixture of howling and baying. Make sure you have tolerant neighbours before this lesson gets under way!

Naturally, a tortvebeller is the finest type of deer-tracking dog as you do not require leads or thongs. However, such dogs are difficult to obtain and it has been found that within a litter only one or two pups will be suitable. Granted dogs will bark, but to sustain barking on command is another thing. It may take you 20 minutes or so to reach the dog whilst it is barking over a deer and it must not stop. It has been calculated that a dog tracking over 700 metres will inhale and exhale 11,000 times. The effort involved is thus considerable and training a dog to concentrate, after this effort, on baying and working unassisted calls for considerable patience on the handler's behalf. However, if you succeed you will have a dog worth its weight in gold.

13

ABOUT THE AUTHORS

DAVID HANCOCK has had a life-long absorption with working dogs. Originally intending to train as a veterinary surgeon, he was deterred by the daily destruction of perfectly healthy pets so changed his mind and entered the Regular Army. This brought him in contact with service dogs: tracking, anti-ambush, patrol and detector-dogs as well as taking him to twenty different countries to study the native and imported working dogs there.

His first book, *Dogs as Companions*, was published in 1981; with *Old Working Dogs* following in 1984. He is well known to dog enthusiasts in this country for his articles in national magazines.

He now works as the Director of the National Trust-owned Shugborough Estate in Staffordshire, which houses the County Museum. He lives in Shropshire where he keeps working sheepdogs. Colonel Hancock has led a full and varied life, going on two Arctic expeditions before he was 21, being 'capped' for England at rugger as a schoolboy and serving with the Light Infantry, the Parachute Regiment and the Gurkhas.

ANGIE LEWIS's career with dogs started when she worked as a kennelmaid in a leading Afghan hound kennels. After her marriage she bred Pembroke corgis, including Ch. Riscoris Red Velvet. In 1968 she became interested in Welsh springer spaniels and was led along the road to gundog competition. As Secretary of the working section of the Welsh springer spaniel club she entered the world of field trials, winning the Minor Breeds Novice Stake three times.

The similarity between Welsh springers and Brittanies led her to acquire her first Brittany spaniel in 1982 and success was achieved in 1984 with her second Brittany dog, Dorvalstan Ulrick of Riscoris when she won awards in hunter-pointer-retriever trials. Since then Angie Lewis has bred, trained and handled the breed's first, and at present, only field trial champion, Riscoris Fleur de Lys. She is currently secretary of the Brittany Club of Great Britain.

SHEILA and **RICHARD KUBAN** bought their first German short-haired pointer in 1968 to work as a gundog and with their goshawks. A few years later they began entering field trials and two of their dogs became field trial champions. Their dogs have always been used for a wide range of sporting activities; rough and walked-up shooting, wildfowling and deerstalking. Although the Kubans do not enter shows regularly, they have had success with several dogs at championship show level. Based in Surrey, they are both on the Kennel Club panel of judges for HPR breeds, and Sheila has been a Field Trial Secretary for 14 years.

MARION JONES, born in 1957, lives in Orpington, Kent. Leaving school at 15, she went straight into a dog-training establishment and from there pursued a career in photography until she began to expand her interest in art. HPRs and, in particular, German wire-haired pointers, are her great love. Completely self-taught, her work is swiftly achieving recognition in the world of sporting art: in 1987 Marion won the Debrett Sporting Artist of the Year Award, and the following year was a 'Natural World' magazine winner at the Society of Wildlife Artists exhibition in London.

GEOFF HARGREAVES began his involvement with HPRs in 1971 with a German short-haired pointer, with which he won the first HPR demonstration competition held at the CLA Game Fair in 1977. Both Geoff and his wife Barbara were founder members of the German short-haired pointer Association and that same teamwork has acquired for their Ghyllbeck affix an enviable reputation in the HPR world for producing quality dogs of outstanding ability. In addition to being a field trial panel judge, Geoff regularly judges championship shows as does his wife, their interest in HPRs being all-embracing.

ANNA COOMBE and **SHEILA GRAY** have been running a boarding kennels in the Midlands since 1987. Before that time Sheila and her late husband, Jim, had been in vizslas for some fifteen years, acquiring two Wolfox bitches, and later, in 1970, importing Futaki Lazslo from the States. From that initial purchase have come a sequence of successful show and working dogs. The authors are now looking forward to the next step in their association with the Hungarian vizsla.

EDWARD HARDMAN was born in Somerset in 1938. After Sandhurst he joined the Royal Tank Regiment in Germany and, following his experiences of wildfowling on the Baltic, developed an interest in Weimaraners which has lasted 30 years. On leaving the army in 1968 he purchased his first Weimaraner and has been working the breed in this country ever since. For the last eight years he has been Field Trials Secretary of the Weimaraner Club of Great Britain and is on the Kennel Club B panel of HPR field trial judges. He has widened his gundog repertoire, winning field trials with Brittanies, and is fortunate that his wife shares his enthusiasm for working gundogs (and indeed does most of the hard work).

As an active worker in dog societies, **BRIAN FINAN** has been a member of the German Short-haired Pointer Association committee and for some time served as working test secretary. He is at present a committee member of the German

Short-haired Pointer Club, serving on both the management and field trial committees. For several years Brian organised and instructed training classes for HPRs in the Lancashire and Cheshire area. He is currently one of the instructors at a training class organised by the Weimaraner Association, near Leeds.

Brenda and Brian Finan have bred and owned dogs under the Geramer's prefix which have been made into Champions, in both GSP and other breeds. The latest Ch. and FT Ch., Geramer's Shannon, was bred by them, one of the very few dual champions in the country. Brian Finan has found success both in the show ring and in field trials, most notably with a GSP Ch. Geramer's Sea Venom ('Blue') which he bred and owned with Brenda. This dog won 23 challenge certificates and 26 field trial awards, including six 1st places.

Finan has served as a judge at working tests, field trials and also in the show ring.

GAY GOTTLIEB was brought up in Buckinghamshire and educated in England, Switzerland and France. She divides her time between her two houses (in London and Hampshire) and the demands of her large family.

Gottlieb has been interested in horses and dogs from an early age. She now breeds, trains, shows and works her own dogs, the well known Russetmantle vizslas. Ch. Russetmantle Troy and Ch. Russetmantle Quiver are but two from her kennel who have won numerous challenge certificates and awards in the field.

Gottlieb's prefix is renowned throughout the gundog world both at home and abroad. She was voted top breeder in the ring from 1982 to 1989. Gottlieb judges the Hungarian vizsla at championship level and is author of the definitive book on the breed, *The Hungarian Vizsla*.

JOHN WAGSTAFF was born in India, in 1940, into a British army family with strong shooting and fishing interests. He therefore developed a great interest in gundogs from an early age. Wagstaff lived in Germany for a period and it was here that his interest in the HPR breeds developed. On settling in England he obtained his first HPR breed, a Large Münsterländer.

From this line he acquired a Large Münsterländer bitch, 'Clara of Abberton', which he was lucky enough to train and make up to the first and only Large Münsterländer FT Ch. in Great Britain to date. Nothing gives him more pleasure than training, trialling and shooting over good HPR dogs.

JOHN HOLMES was born in 1928 and was brought up in the rural South Midlands. After leaving school, and a period spent in National Service, he qualified as a vet in London in December 1954. He then spent six years in country practice in Lincolnshire, Leicestershire and Devon. After experience in small animal and equine practice on the south coast, he founded his own practice in 1963 and has since specialised in gundog injuries and homeopathic medicine. He has been Honorary Veterinary Surgeon to the Weimaraner Club of Great Britain for 20 years.

Holmes's early sporting interests – county class rugby, athletics and hockey – were followed by field sports: shooting, fly fishing and HPR training. He has spent 10 years on local radio and presented a programme on household pets for the BBC. He works Weimaraners and German wire-haired pointers on the shooting scene, continuing his lifelong association with working dogs.

DIANA DURMAN-WALTERS has been involved with gundog training at her Scottish kennels for the past decade. She is, in addition, co-director of the Scottish Academy of Falconry and Related Studies. Her special interest is in German wire-haired pointers and she has one of the best known kennels of imported working dogs from Germany: "Wiggmansburg" stock have embellished some of the most auspicious country homes in Great Britain, as well as being exported world-wide.

Diana has trained an extensive variety of gundogs for clients requiring them for shooting, stalking, falconry and field trials.

With the increase in interest in falconry, Diana's professional skills in training are being fully utilised. With the magnificent border country to train in it is no surprise that many talented dogs have passed through her hands. Indeed, it is here that she can indulge in her other great passion of falconry. Diana has featured on television and radio and is a familiar figure at game fairs, with her falcon-flying displays.

14

BREED SOCIETIES

Brittany Club of Great Britain:
Mrs E. Hughes, Hill House, Iron Acton, Bristol, Avon BS17 1XA
Tel: 045 422 493

German Short-haired Pointer Association:
Mrs B. Rigby, The Paddocks, Wigsley Rd, North Scarle, Lincoln LN6 99HD
Tel: 0527 7613

German Short-haired Pointer Club:
Mrs V. Grant, 30 Morritt Avenue, Leeds LS15 7EP
Tel: 0532 600120

German Wire-haired Pointer Club:
Miss S. Pinkerton, Bareve, Old Station House, Caldecott, Market Harborough,
Leicestershire
Tel: 0536 770714

Hungarian Vizsla Club:
Mrs H. F. Gould, Red Tiles, Ravens Green, Little Bentley, Colchester CO7 8TA
Tel: 0206 250327

Hungarian Vizsla Society:
Mrs S. Gray, 261 High Lane East, West Hallam, Derbyshire DE7 6HZ
Tel: 0602 322763

Large Münsterländer Club:
Mrs E. Tyson, Gorsebank House, Eckington Rd, New Whittington, Chesterfield,
Derbyshire
Tel: 0246 450 892

Weimaraner Club of Great Britain:
Mrs P. LeMon, 6 The Glebe, Cuxton, Rochester, Kent ME2 1LW
Tel: 0634 710915